METAPHYSICS

Books VII–X

ARISTOTLE

METAPHYSICS

BOOKS VII–X

Zeta, Eta, Theta, Iota

Translated by

Montgomery Furth

HACKETT PUBLISHING COMPANY

Designed by Mark E. Van Halsema
Cover design by Jackie Lacy
Typeset by Publishers Service, Bozeman, Montana

For further information address
Hackett Publishing Company, Inc.
P.O. Box 44937
Indianapolis, Indiana 46204

Library of Congress Cataloging in Publication Data

Aristotle.
    Metaphysics. Books zeta, eta, theta, iota (VII–X).

    Translation of: Metaphysica, books 7–10.
    1. Metaphysics—Early works to 1800. I. Furth,
Montgomery. II. Title.
B434.A5F87 1984   110   84-19159
ISBN 0–915145–89–8 (alk. paper)
ISBN 0–915145–90–1 (pbk. : alk. paper)

Translator's Preface

There already exists a good English translation of the *Metaphysics*, that of Ross. Why then put forward the concoction that follows? Because for some purposes, a good English translation is not what is needed.

The aim of this rendering of four of the central books is to make available to the reader as exactly and as literally as possible what is in Aristotle's text as we have it. No translation can simultaneously attain that aim and be in good English; Aristotle's text is terse and elliptical, and reads like cipher. Here is one famous sample:

> And first, let us say a few things about it formulawise, that the what it is to be of each thing is that which is said in respect of itself. For the being for you is not the being for musical; for you are not musical in respect of yourself. Therefore, that which in respect of yourself. (Zeta 4)

Faced with this sort of thing, translators endeavor to bridge the gap between it and English by *interpolating* in the light of their understanding of its meaning and their sense of diction and style. That is a necessary enterprise, and it has been creditably, sometimes brilliantly done, but the consequence is nonetheless paraphrase, in which the divide between data and interpretation is effaced. For philosophical study of such a work as this, the reader, not just the translator, should know what the translator was looking at when he or she began to interpolate. In the present version, all else is sacrificed to that central aim. No literary virtues are to be found here, and where some interpolation is required (as it constantly is; the sample above is typical as well as famous), either of matter obviously implied but not stated, or of an exegetical character, everything added is in square brackets [ ]. The result is not pretty, but in this way the aptness of anything added is open to scrutiny and criticism. My goal has been to make a version that presents just what the Greek text presents, that delivers the difficulties therein just as they are without tacitly deciding them, and that engenders in the reader of this so far as possible the same mental condition as the original engenders in the reader of that.

The rest of this preface explains some of the background to the present piece and a few other prefatory matters.

From time to time over the past fifteen years, in the course of composing an extended work on Aristotle's theory of material substances, I have made translations for my own use of some of the more vexed passages in the Aristotelian corpus, which were either linguistically or philosophically (or both) too difficult for my limited linguistic and philosophical competences to deal with simultaneously. As is natural for such a purpose, these renderings were as literal as possible, indeed to the point of rebarbativeness or even barbarity; but no harm in that, since no one's literary sensibility was at risk but my own, which was already suspect in any case as that responsible for the atrocities themselves. However, being accustomed to share whatever aids to understanding might be at my disposal with my students, I made these available to them, and presently added further translations as their usefulness seemed indicated. Sometime in the mid-1970s, I filled in the remaining gaps to make a complete version of *Metaphysics* Zeta and Eta; by that time, the spirit of merciless literalness of the translation had long been evoked as "a rendering from Aristotle's Greek, into a vernacular neither English nor Greek, called Eek", and the version had been styled The Eek Papers. It has circulated, in *samizdat* fashion, to various graduate departments in this country and Canada and has been used by students and professional colleagues to ends similar to my own;

and I have revised it occasionally in response to valuable feedback from several sources.

There the matter stood for some time, except that a rendering of Theta was added in 1983, mostly for my own benefit in the monograph composition as of that time. Throughout I have considered the translation to be fundamentally a teaching aid rather than a contribution to scholarship; and I spurned suggestions that it be published, for two main reasons. One was a feeling that published works ought to be in some language recognized in the civilized world, such as English or Chinese, and not in uncouth pidgins, such as Eek; though this line of thought did lose some of its force when an Eek translation of the *Posterior Analytics* by Jonathan Barnes was published in 1975. The other was that I had neither will nor resource to make the full annotation that a proper version required, on the model of the Clarendon Aristotle Series, which represents for all who work these vineyards in the English-speaking world the state of the art.

However, Hackett Publishing Company's suggestion of publication in the present format seemed quite reasonable. The Hackett imprint connotes editions of quality of philosophical classics, not necessarily heavily edited and annotated, for undergraduate and graduate study at reasonable cost. In such a setting I am happy to make the version available in the hope that it may be of use to a more aboveground audience than has shared it to date. A translation of Iota has been added, and a glossary of the standard renderings of technical and other important terms.

The only significant remaining question has concerned the notes. As a consequence of the circumstances of the version's production, the distribution of notes in the Eek Papers was highly uneven; certain chapters were quite extensively commented on (e.g., Zeta 4, 6, 7, 10, 11, 17; Eta 1, 2), others, equally in need thereof, scarcely at all. As already indicated, I had no intention of trying to annotate the entirety, and have therefore had to choose between leaving the lopsided treatment as of the latest metamorphic recension of the Eek, and suppressing the fuller elucidatory notes in the interest of uniformity. With hesitation, I have at last opted for the former. Notes are especially scarce in Theta and Iota. However, if the work proves useful further printings are anticipated, in which over time this and other shortcomings can to some extent be alleviated. Nothing could be more welcome than criticisms and other suggestions to that end.

Ross's text (*Aristotle's Metaphysics*, Oxford, 1953) is followed except as indicated, and his commentary is cited as *AM*. "OCT" is the Oxford Classical Text of Jaeger (*Aristotelis Metaphysica*, Oxford, 1963). In both translation and notes, the Bekker page numbers 1028^a-1059^a are abbreviated as 28^a-59^a, and in the translation, an asterisk * indicates a note, while a degree mark ° indicates the first occurrence of terms listed in the Glossary. Neither books nor chapters are titled in the original text; the chapter titles here are my invention, and the table of contents gives one possible view of the organization of the whole.

I am much indebted to David Blank and Nicholas White, who made detailed comments on the penultimate draft, and again to Blank for much helpful consultation in the final phase. I have accepted many of their suggestions, but where even they could not save me I am alone responsible. The experience has also taught me anew, as it must anyone who tries such a thing as this, how very good the Ross translation is.

Contents

Z

Zeta 1 [That which 'is' in the primary sense is substance.]

28ᵃ10 *Being* or *that which is*°* is said°* in many ways°, as we went through earlier in our remarks 'on the number of ways°' [in which things are said] [cf. Delta 7]; for it signifies, on one hand, the 'what it is'° and 'some this'°, and on the other hand, the 'so-qualified'° or the 'so-much'° or each of the other things-predicated° as these are. **ᵃ13** But though *what is* is said in so many ways as this, it's evident that primary° among these is the 'what it is', for it's that which signifies the substance° (for when we're saying how-qualified this thing is, we say [it's] good, or bad, but not three-cubits, or man; but when [we're saying] what it is, [we say] not pale, or hot, or three-cubits, but man, or god); but the others are called beings by way of being, some, quantities of what *is* in this sense, others, qualities, others again, afflictions°, still others, something else.

28ᵃ20 For this reason, someone might even raise the aporia°* whether *walking* and *being healthy* and *sitting* signified each of them a *being*, and likewise too for everything else of this sort; for none of these either is by its nature 'in respect of itself'°, or is capable of being-separated° from the substance, but rather, if anything, it's the walker [= the walking substance] that belongs among the *beings*, and the sitter, and the healthy [one]. **ᵃ25** These latter seem more to be beings, because there is something which is for them a determinate° subject° (and this is the substance and the particular°), which is just what is made manifest in this sort of predication; for *the good* [*thing*] or *the sitter* are not said without this.

28ª29. It's clear, then, that it is on account of this [= substance] that each of those other things *is*, so that that which *is* primarily°, i.e. not 'is something', but 'is, *simpliciter*°', would be substance. **ª31** Now, *primary* is said in many ways; but nevertheless substance is primary in all of them, both [1] in formula° and [2] in knowledge° and [3] in time°. **ª33** For [3] none of the other [types of] things-predicated is *separate*°, only this [= substance] alone; and [1] in formula this is primary (for necessarily in the formula of each thing, that of the substance is present); and [2] we think we know each thing most of all, when we know *what* man is, [for example,] or fire, more than the so-qualified or the **28ᵇ** so-much or the where, since even of these latter, we know each one when we know *what* the so-much is, or the so-qualified.*

28ᵇ2 And moreover, what is sought after both long ago and now and always, and always puzzled over [*aporoumenon*]: *what is being?*—is just [the question], *what is substance?* (for this some say is one, others more than one, and of the latter, some say is limited, others unlimited); for which reason it is for us too to investigate ["theorize"] most of all, and primarily, even—so to speak—exclusively, concerning that which *is* in this way [= substance], what it is.

Zeta 2 [Some views as to what sorts of things are substance.]

28ᵇ8 Substance seems to belong° [1] most obviously to bodies (which is why we say that the animals, and the plants, and their parts, are substances; also, the 'natural° bodies', such as fire and water and earth and each thing of that sort; also, such things as are parts of these or are 'out of'° them, whether of some or of all, such as the universe° [lit., "heaven"] and its parts, stars and moon and sun).* But whether these alone are substances or there are also others, or just some of these, or [some of these and] also others, or *none* of these but *only* others, must be looked into.

28ᵇ16 [2] To some it seems that 'the *limits* of body', such as plane and line and point and unit° [*monas*], are substances, more so than body and the solid.

28ᵇ18 Further, [3] besides° [*para*] perceptible° things some people don't think there is anything of that sort; but [4] others [think that] there *are* more things, which are 'more beings' and are eternal, in the way that Plato [thinks] the forms° and the mathematika° are two [kinds of] substances, and a third is the substance of the perceptible bodies; and [5] Speusippus—even more substances, starting off° from the one, and 'first principles°' of each [kind of] substance, one of numbers, another of magnitudes, yet another of the soul°; and going on in this way he extends the [kinds of] substances. **ᵇ24** [6] And then some say [= Xenocrates?] that the forms and the numbers have the *same* nature°, and the others come along next—lines and planes—right up to the substance of the [physical] universe [*ouranos*] and [up to] the perceptibles.

28ᵇ27 Regarding these things, then, [i] what is said well or not well, and [ii] which things are substances, and [iii] whether there are any besides the perceptible ones, or not, and [iv] *how* these [= perceptible substances] are, and [v] whether there is any substance that's *separate*, and if so why or how, or whether there is none, besides the perceptibles, must be looked into; and we must first sketch out substance, what it is.

Zeta 3   [Analysis (I). Substance as under-lying, or sub-ject (hypokeimenon).]

28ᵇ33 Substance is said, if not in more ways, at least chiefly in four: that is, [1] the essence° and [2] the universal° and [3] the genus° seem to be the substance of each thing, and fourthly, the subject* of these.

28ᵇ36 The 'subject' is 'that of which° the other things are said, but which itself is never [said] of any other thing'. So first **29ᵃ** a determination° must be made about this; for the primary subject seems most of all to be substance.*

29ᵃ2 Now in one way the matter° is said to be of this sort [= a subject], in another way the shape°, and in a third way what is 'out of' these—I mean by "the matter", e.g. the bronze; by "the shape", the configuration° of what is seen; by "what's 'out of these'", the statue, i.e. the composite°. **ᵃ5** So that if the form° is prior° to the matter and more a being, it will also be prior to what's 'out of' both of them, for the same reason.

29ᵃ7 Now then, it has been said in outline what substance is, that it's 'that which isn't [said] *of* a subject, but *of* which the other things [are said]'; but *this* can't be all, for it is not enough; for this itself is unclear, and beyond that, the *matter* becomes substance. **ᵃ10** For if this [= the matter] is not substance, it escapes us what else is. For the other things being stripped off*, nothing [else] seems to be left over. For the other things are afflictions and products and potentialities° of bodies, or again length and breadth and depth are particular quantities [of bodies] but not substances—for the so-much is not substance—but rather, that primary thing to which these *belong, that* is substance. **ᵃ16** But length and breadth and depth being stripped off, we see nothing left over—unless it be something that is demarcated by the agency of° these, so that the matter alone necessarily seems to be substance to those who are investigating in this way.

29ᵃ20 I call matter that which, in its own right°, is neither said to be something [*ti*] nor so-much nor any of the other things by which being is demarcated. **ᵃ21** For there is something of which each of these is predicated, something for which *being* [*to einai*] is other than what it is for any of the [other] predicates (for the others are predicated of the substance, but the substance itself is predicated of the matter), so that the last [member of this sequence, i.e. the matter] is, in its own right, neither something [*ti*] nor so-much nor anything else; nor is it the negations [of these], for these too will belong *per accidens*°.

29ᵃ26 Well then, for those considering along these lines, it results that the matter is substance; but this is impossible; for in fact '*separate*' and '*this*' seem to belong above all to substance, for which reason, the form and what's 'out of' the two would more seem to be substance than the matter. **ᵃ30** The substance that's 'out of' the two, though, I mean the one that's 'out of' the matter and the shape, should be set aside, for it's posterior°, and clear; and the matter too is in a sense evident; but the third has got to be investigated, for *that* is *most* puzzling [*aporōtatē*].

29ᵃ33 It is agreed that there are some substances among perceptible things, so that inquiry should first be made among these. **29ᵇ3** For it forwards the work to proceed toward what is more knowable. For learning takes place for all in this way, through things less knowable by nature toward those more knowable; and just as in the case of our actions, [the task is] from that which is good for each, to make things that are entirely good be good for each, —in just the same way, this is our task: from things that are more known to oneself, to make things that are more knowable by nature also more known to oneself. **ᵇ8** But the things that are known and primary for particular persons, are very often hardly knowable, and have little or no being in them; but all the same, from what is barely known but known to oneself, one must try to know things that are entirely know-able, proceeding, just as has been said, through these [things that are known to oneself].*

Zeta 4 [Analysis (II). Substance as essence.]

29ᵇ1 Since at the start we went through how many ways we define substance, and of these one seems to be the essence*, this needs to be thought over.

[1. 1029^{b}13-16 "Essence" of X as what X is 'in respect of itself'.]

29^{b}13* And first, let us say a few things about it that hold good for it from its formula° [*logikōs*], to wit, that the essence for each thing is that which is said [of it] [or: what it is said to be] 'in respect of itself' [*kath' hauto*]. **^{b}14** For, *being you$_d$*° is not [the same as] *being musical$_d$**, for you are not musical 'in respect of yourself' [*kata sauton*]*. What you are 'in respect of yourself', then [—*that* is your essence].

[2. 1029^{b}16-1030^{a}2 Trying to fix the relevant sense of 'in respect of itself'.]

29^{b}16 Yet this is not all; for that which is 'in respect of itself' in this way isn't the way pale [belongs] to surface ['in respect of itself'], because *being a surface$_d$* isn't [the same as] *being pale$_d$*.

29^{b}18 Nor, again, is what is 'out of' the two, *being a pale$_d$ surface$_d$* [a case of 'in respect of itself' being as meant here], because of the addition [of *pale$_d$*].*

29^{b}19 Therefore, the formula in which the thing isn't actually present, but which *formulates* it ["says it"], this is the formula of the essence for each thing*, so that if *being a pale$_d$ surface$_d$* is [= were, e.g.] *being a smooth$_d$ surface$_d$*, then *being pale$_d$* and *being smooth$_d$* are [= would be] the same and one.

29^{b}22 But since there are also compounds°* made by way of the other categories (for there is some subject for each one, e.g. for the so-qualified, and the so-much, and the at-some-time and the at-some-place and the motion°), it must be looked into whether there is a 'formula of the essence' for each one of these, and does the 'esssence' belong to these too,—for example, to [a] *pale man*.—**^{b}27** Let a name for this be *cloak*. What is *to be* [a] *cloak$_d$*?—But surely, this too is *not* something that is said 'in respect of itself'.

29^b29 Or: is "not 'in respect of itself'." said in two ways, [i] one from something being attached [*ek prostheseōs*], [ii] the other not? **b31** For [i] in one case, what's being defined is said by the fact that '*it-[X]-attaches-to-something-else-[Y]*', e.g. if a person defining *being pale*_d were to say the formula of [a] *pale*_a*man*; [ii] in the other case, [it's said in the form] '*another thing attaching to this*', e.g. if "cloak" meant [a] pale man, but he were to define cloak as pale_a. [30^a] That is, pale_a man is indeed pale_a, but not, however, the essence for *being pale*_d.*

[3. 1030^a2-17 The "interior of the essence". Essence as *hoper* some genus, i.e. species of a genus, as opposed to 'one thing of another'.]

30^a2 But is *being a cloak*_d any essence at all? Or not? For the essence is *hoper*° some [G]; but when something is said of some *other* thing, that is not *hoper* some this, e.g. the pale man isn't *hoper* some this, at any rate if the 'this' belongs only to substances; so that the essence would be of such things whose formula is a *definition*° [*horismos*].*

30^a7 —Definition is not [just] a name meaning the same as a formula, (for then all formulae would be definitions, for there will be a name answering to any formula whatsoever, so that even the Iliad will be a definition*), but only if it is [definition] *of* something primary; and of this sort are such things as are said *not* by way of saying something of something *else* [*allo kat' allou*].

30^a11 It follows that the essence cannot belong to anything but the species [pl.] of a genus* and to them alone (for these seem *not* to be said by way of a 'participation°' or 'affliction', nor 'as accident'); i.e., there will be a formula of each of the other things also, [formulating] what each signifies— provided there is a name, namely [a formula saying] that *this* belongs to *this*, or instead of a simple° formula a more exact one; but these *won't* be definition, nor essence either.

[4. 1030ᵃ17-ᵇ3 Manyness of 'essence' and 'referred' being.]

30ᵃ17 Or is definition too, like the 'what it is', said in more than one way°? For the 'what it is', taken in one way, means the substance and the 'some this'*, but taken in another way, [means] each of the other things-predicated: so-much and so-qualified and the others like that. **ᵃ21** For just as *is* too belongs to each of them, but not in the same way, rather to one primarily and the others derivatively, so too the 'what it is' belongs to substance *simpliciter*, and to the others after a fashion; in fact, of the so-qualified we may ask 'what it is', so that so-qualified too is a 'what a thing is', but not *simpliciter*, rather in just the way that some people say in the case of 'what is not' that, going by the formula [*logikōs*], "what is not, is", not 'is' *simpliciter*, but 'is' what is not—so too with the so-qualified.

30ᵃ27 One must, then, also examine how one must speak of each [of these cases], but of course no more so than how things actually are; and so now too, since what is *said* is evident, the essence too will belong primarily and *simpliciter* to substance, and secondarily ["then"] to the others, in just the same way as does 'what it is', not *simpliciter*, but essence-for-quality, or for-quantity. **ᵃ32** For necessarily either these are 'beings' homonymously°, or else by adding and taking away, just as the unknown is known*, since what's correct is that they're said [to be beings] *neither* homonymously, *nor* in exactly the same way, but like the *medical*: in that [all these 'beings' are said] *with reference to* one and **30ᵇ** the same thing° [*pros to auto kai hen*], not that it ['being', or 'medical'] *is* one and the same thing, nor a homonym either; for medical body, and procedure, and apparatus are said not homonymously, nor *in respect of* one thing° [*kath' hen*] but *with reference to* one thing [*pros hen*]*.

[5. 1030^{b}3-13 Summary restatement of (3) and (4).]

30^{b}3 —But it makes no difference in which one of the two ways one wishes to say these things*; this is plain: that which primarily and *simpliciter* is definition, and the essence, belong to the substances. **30^{b}6** Not that they don't belong to the other things likewise, only not primarily.* For it's not necessary, if we stipulate this, that a definition of this be whatever name signifies the same thing as a formula, but as a certain [type of] formula; this [being the case] if it is [the formula] of *one* thing, not [one] by continuity like the Iliad or things [that are one] by being tied together, but [if it is one] in the ways one is said; **^{b}10** —*one* is said like *being*; *being* means on the one hand, 'some this', and on the other hand, quantity, some quality, etc. **^{b}12** Which is why there can be a formula and definition even of [a] pale$_a$ man, only in a different way from one of the pale$_{[n?]}$, and from one of [a] substance.

Zeta 5 ['Coupled' terms.]

30^{b}14 There is an aporia: if one does not call the formula that 'arises out of an attachment' a definition [cf. Zeta 4 29^{b}30], of which of the things that are not simple but 'coupled'° [fastened-together, *syndedyasmena*] can there be definition?; for they can only be explained as 'out of attachment'. **^{b}16** I mean, for example, there is *nose* and *concavity*, and then *snubness*, which is said as arising 'out of the first two', the second in the first, and it's not per accidens that either the concavity or the snubness is an affliction of the nose, but in respect of itself*;—not in the way that pale stands to Callias, or to [a] man—because Callias is pale, who it happens is a man—but instead as male to animal, or as equal to quantity, and as all things [are] which are said to belong in respect of themselves.* **b23** These are the things in which is present either the formula or the name of that *of* which this is the affliction, and which cannot be explained apart from° [*khōris*] that: in the way that pale can be [explained] without man, but not female without animal; **b26** so that of any of these things either there is no essence and definition, or, if there is, it's in a different way, just as we've said [cf. Zeta 4 30ª17-ᵇ13].

30ᵇ28 But there's also another aporia about these. For if *snub nose* and *concave nose* are the same, then *snub* and *concave* will be the same; but if they're not [the same], on the grounds that it's impossible to say *snub* without the thing *of* which it's an affliction in respect of itself—for snub *is* concavity *in a nose*—, then to say *snub nose* either is impossible or else the same thing will have been said twice over, *concave-nose nose*—for the 'snub' nose will be 'concave nose' nose—for which reason it's absurd that essence should belong to things like this; if it does, it will go on indefinitely; for in a snub nose nose there will be yet **31ª** another [nose].

31ª1 It's plain, accordingly, that there can be definition of substance alone. For if [there is definition] of the other kinds of thing-predicated too, it has got to be 'from an attachment', as with [definition] of the even and odd*, which can't be done without number, nor female without animal (I mean by "from attachment", the cases in which it turns out that the same thing is said twice over, as in the cases here). **a5** But if this is true, then neither can there be any [definition] of coupled things° [*syndyazomena*], such as *odd number*; but this escapes notice because the formulae don't formulate precisely. **a7** But if there are definitions of these things too, then either they're [made] in a different way, or else, as was said before, definition and essence must be said in many ways, so that in *one* way there can be no definition nor can essence belong to anything except for substances, but in *another* way there can be [definition and essence for other things].

31ᵃ11 It's plain, then, that [i] definition is the formula of the essence, and [ii] the essence is either of substances alone, or of them chiefly and primarily and *simpliciter*.*

Zeta 6 [What things are identical with their essences?]

31ᵃ15 It must be inquired into whether each thing and [its] essence are the same or different. For this will somewhat advance the inquiry about substance; for [a] each thing is thought not to be *other* than its own substance, and [b] the essence is said to be the substance of each thing.

31ᵃ19 [I.] Now, in the case of things that are said per accidens it would seem that the two are different, e.g. a pale man different from the essence of pale man (for if they were the same, then the essence of man and the essence of pale man would be the same; for a man and a pale man are the same, as they say [that is, if he's in fact pale], so that the essence of pale man and that of man [will be the same] also*; —or is it *not* necessary that the things that are per accidens be the same? —for the extreme terms [in the preceding argument] don't become the same [as the middle term] in the same *way*; —but perhaps *this* might be thought to follow° [*symbainein*]: that the per accidens things which are the extremes become the same, in the manner of, e.g., essence of pale and essence of musical?* But no, it seems not).*

31ᵃ28 [II.] In the case of things that are said in respect of themselves, however, is it necessary that [a thing] be the same [as its essence], for instance if there exist some substances to which no substances or any other natures are *prior*, things such as some people say the ideas° are? **ᵃ31** —For if the good-itself [*auto to agathon*] and the essence of good are going to be different, also animal and the essence of animal, and the essence of being and being, **31ᵇ** then there are going to be other substances and natures and ideas beyond those that were mentioned, and those others will be both prior and more substance*—if the essence is substance. **ᵇ3** And if they [the ideas and the essences] are detached from one another, then [a] there can be no knowledge of the [ideas] nor [b] can [the essences] be beings (I mean by "being detached", if neither does the essence of good belong to the good-itself, nor does it belong to [the essence of good] *to be good*). **ᵇ6** —[a] For it is knowledge of each thing when we know the essence of that thing*, and [b] what holds for *good* holds for the others, so that if not even the essence of good is good, neither will the essence of being be a being, nor the essence of one be one; **ᵇ9** in the same way, either all the essences are, or none, so that if the essence of being is not a being, then none of the others is either. **ᵇ11** —Again, that to which the essence of good does not belong, is not good.

31ᵇ11 Necessarily, then, the good and essence of good are one, and so are fair and essence of fair, and so with all things that are not said in respect of another [*kat' allo*], but in respect of themselves [*kath' hauta*] and primary*; **ᵇ14** for it is even enough if this [condition] applies, even if they aren't forms [*eidē*], or rather perhaps even if they *are* forms (**ᵇ15** at the same time it is also clear that on the assumption that there are ideas such as some people say, then the subject won't be substance; for these [the ideas] necessarily are substances, but are not [predicated] *of* a subject; for [sc. if that were so] they will *be* by being partaken of).

31ᵇ18 From these arguments, then, each-thing-itself [*auto hekaston*, i.e. each idea] and its essence are one and the same, and not [so] per accidens; also because to *understand* each thing is just to understand the essence, so that even by *ekthesis* the two are necessarily one thing*; but what is said per accidens, like musical or pale, owing to its having a double signification it is not true to say that it and the essence are the same; indeed, both that on which pale supervenes [accidit] and the supervener [accident] [are called *pale*], so that in one way it [pale] and the essence are the same and in another not the same; for the essence of man and the essence of pale men are not the same, but it [pale] is the same as the essence of the affliction [pale].*

31ᵇ28 Absurdity would become apparent also [in separating such things and their essences] if one assigned a name to each of the essences; for over and above [*para*] *this* one, there will be another, for the essence of e.g. horse [there will be] another essence. Yet what prevents some things' being their essence right from the start?—if, that is, essence is substance?

31ᵇ32 But in fact, not only are they one, but their **32ᵃ** formula is also the same, as is clear from what's been said; for it's not per accidens that one and the essence of one are one. Furthermore, if they're to be distinct, it goes on indefinitely; for on one hand there will be essence of one, and on the other hand the one—so that the same argument [*logos*] will apply to the former things too.

32ᵃ4 It's clear, then, that in the case of the things that are said in respect of themselves and primary, X and the essence of X are the same and one; and the sophistical elenchuses° against this thesis are evidently solved by the same solution, **ᵃ8** as is [the question] whether Socrates and essence of Socrates are the same; for there's no difference either in the components from which one would construct the question, or in those from which one would obtain a successful solution.

32ᵃ10 In what way, then, the essence is the same as each thing and in what way not, has been said.*

Zeta 7 [Coming-to-be.]*

32ᵃ12 Of things that come-to-be°, some come-to-be by nature°, some by art°, and some from their own agency°; but all things that come-to-be, come-to-be

[a] by the agency of something, and
[b] out of something, and

[c] [come to be] something/somewhat [*ti*];
and the something/somewhat which I say [they come-to-be]
may be of any category; for [they come-to-be] *this*, or so-
much or so-qualified or so-located.*

32ª16 Now, the *'natural'* comings-to-be° [*geneses*] are
those of the things whose coming-to-be is 'out of nature', and
there is [b] that 'out of which' they come-to-be, which we
call 'matter', and [a] that 'by whose agency' [they come-to-
be] is some thing that exists naturally, and [c] the some-
thing/somewhat [they come-to-be]* is [a] *man* or [a] *plant*
or something else like these, which we say to be substances
most of all. **ª20** —All things that come-to-be either by nature or by art have matter; for each of them is capable both
of being and of not-being, and this is the matter in each
one*—and generally, both that out of which [things come-
to-be] is a nature, and that in respect of which° [*kath' ho*]
[they come-to-be] is a nature—for what comes-to-be *has* a
nature, e.g. *plant* or *animal*,*—and likewise for that by-
whose-agency [they come-to-be]: what is called *the nature
in respect of the form**, which is specifically identical
[*homo-eides*] (though this is in another); for human being
generates° human being.

32ª25 Thus, then, come-to-be the things that come-to-be
through nature; the other comings-to-be are called 'makings' [*poiēseis*]. And all makings are either from art or from
a power° or from thought. Some of them come-to-be also
spontaneously and from chance, exactly as with the things
that come-to-be from nature; for there, too, some of the
same things come-to-be both out of seed, and without
seed.* Concerning these, then, inquiry must be made
later*; but from art **32ᵇ** come-to-be the things whose form is
in the soul [of the maker]—I call *form* the Essence of each
thing and the Primary Substance; for in a certain sense even
contraries° can have the same form; for the substance of the
lack° is the opposite substance, e.g. health of disease, for
disease 'is' by the absence [*apousia*] of health*, where the

health is the formula in the soul, the knowledge. **ᵇ6** The healthy [thing] comes-to-be when one [= the physician] reasons° as follows: since health is *this* [*todi*], necessarily if [the thing] is to be healthy, *this* must be present—say, 'a uniform state' — and if that [is to be present], then 'heat'— and he goes on always thinking like this, until he is led to a final 'this' which he himself is able to make. **ᵇ9** Then the movement [*kinēsis*] from this point forward is called a 'making'—that is, the [movement] toward being-healthy. **ᵇ11** So that it follows that in a certain sense the health comes to be out of health, and the house out of house: that which has matter [from] that without matter; for the medical art and the house-building art are the form of the health and of the house, and by "substance without matter", I mean the Essence.

32ᵇ15 Of the comings-to-be and movements, one is called "thinking"° [*noēsis*] and the other "making" [*poiēsis*]; *thinking* is the one [that proceeds] from the starting-point° [*arkhē*] and the form [e.g., "health is *this*", ᵇ6-7 above], and *making* is the one [proceeding] from the completing° stage of the thinking. **ᵇ17** And each of the other things in between comes-to-be in the same way. I mean, for example, if he is to be healthy, then he would need to be-made-uniform. Then what is being-made-uniform? It's *this*, and this will come about if he is made warm. **ᵇ20** The latter, then, what's that? It's *this*. But *this* is present potentially°*, and that is already within his [= the physician's] power.

32ᵇ21 The maker [*poioun*], then, and that whence begins the movement of becoming-healthy [the "starting point" of ᵇ16], if it happens from art, is the form that is in the soul; but if it happens spontaneously, then it's 'from' whatever it is that starts the making for the maker 'from' art, just as in healing perhaps the starting-point is 'from' *heating* (and this he makes by rubbing). **ᵇ26** So either the warmth in the body, then, is a part of the health or else something similar ["uniformity"?, cf. ᵇ7, 19] follows it [= the warmth] which is part of the health, either [following] immediately or by way of more than one step*; and this, the maker of the part of health, is the final thing; **ᵇ29** —and so too with the house (e.g. the ["final thing" is] the stones), and with the other cases.*

32ᵇ30 So that, as they say, 'coming-to-be were impossible if nothing were present beforehand'.*

32ᵇ31 That *some* part necessarily [pre-]exists, then, is evident; for the matter is a part, (for it is this that is present within, **33ª** and comes-to-be [something/somewhat, cf. 32ª14, 18]). Well then, but is it also any of the things in the formula? Well, we certainly say of *brazen circles* 'what they are' in both ways: saying both of the matter 'that it's bronze', and of the form 'that it's this sort of figure', and this [= 'figure', *skhēma*] is the genus in which it's first placed. **ª4** The *brazen circle*, then, does have the matter in its formula.

33ª5 As for that 'out of which' as matter they come-to-be, some are said, when once they've come-to-be, to be not *that* but *thaten*, e.g. the statue is not *stone* but *stonen* [not *lithos* but *lithinos*]; and the man, i.e. the healthy man, is not said to be *that* 'out of which' [he has come-to-be] [that]. **ª8** The reason is that he comes-to-be 'out of' both the lack and the substrate, which we call the matter—e.g., it's both *the man* and *the sick* [one] that come-to-be healthy—; however, it's really much more said to come-to-be out of the lack, as, 'out of a sick [one], a healthy', rather than out of man; which is why the healthy [one] isn't called sick, but is called a man, and the man is called healthy. **ª13** But as for things where the lack is unclear or has no name—such as in bronze, [the lack of] whatever configuration, or in bricks & timbers, [the lack of] house, 'out of' these they [statue, house] seem to come-to-be in the way that in the other case [the healthy one comes-to-be] from the sick; **ª16** which is why, just as in the other case the thing is not called *that*, 'out of which' [it comes-to-be], so here the statue is not called wood, but rather takes on a derived term, *wooden**, and *brazen* but not *bronze*, and *stonen* but not *stone*, [a19] and the house: *bricken* but not *bricks*—since it also isn't the case that 'out of' wood a statue comes-to-be, or 'out of' bricks a house, if one were to examine the question carefully, he wouldn't say it *simpliciter*, because coming-to-be requires a change° [*metaballontos*] in the 'out of which', but not that it remain. [a23] This, then, is the reason why it is said in this way.*

Zeta 8 [Form does not come-to-be, any more than matter, only the "composite".]

[33a24] Since that which comes-to-be, comes-to-be
- [a] by the agency of something (and this I call the 'starting-point whence' of the coming-to-be), and
- [b] out of something (and let this be, not the lack, but the matter; for it's already been explained [Z 7 end] what we mean by this), and
- [c] comes-to-be something/somewhat (and this is either a sphere or a circle or whatever of the others it may happen to be),

just as he doesn't make the substrate, the bronze, so in the same way neither [does he make] the sphere, except per accidens in that the brazen sphere is [a] sphere, and the former he does make. [a31] For, *to make some this* [*tode ti poiein*] is, *out of a subject in the full sense of the phrase to make some this*—I mean, *to make the bronze round* is not to make the round or the sphere but something different, viz., *this form in another*; for if he does make [the form], [33b] he would have to make it out of something other, for this underlay [or: this was assumed?]*; e.g., he makes a brazen sphere, and that in the following sense: *out of THIS*, which is bronze, *he makes THIS*, which is [a] sphere; [b3] —if, then, he also makes this [*sc.* the form] itself, clearly he'll make that in the same fashion, and the comings-to-be will regress to infinity.

ᵇ5 It is evident, therefore, that the form, or whatever the shape [*morphē*] that's in the perceptible thing should be called, does not come-to-be, nor is there any coming-to-be of it, nor does the Essence [come-to-be]—it is this that comes-to-be in another [cf. 33ᵃ34 above], whether by agency of art or by agency of nature or a power [Zeta 7 32ᵃ28]. **ᵇ8** But *there being a brazen sphere, this* he makes; for he makes it 'out of' *bronze* and *sphere*; for in *this* he makes the form*, and the result is a brazen sphere. **ᵇ11** But if there is going to be a coming-to-be of the Essence of sphere in general, then something will have to be 'out of' something. For that which comes-to-be will always have to be divisible, and be 'on one hand this, on the other hand that'; I mean, 'on one hand matter, on the other hand form'. **ᵇ14*** If, then, *sphere* is *figure equidistant from the center*, then of this one part is *that in which* what he makes will be, and the other part is what is *in that*, and the whole is what has come-to-be—like the brazen sphere. **ᵇ16** It's evident, then, from what has been said, that what is called the form or substance does not come-to-be, but that the composite [*synolon*], i.e. what is called with respect to this, does come-to-be, and that in every thing that is generated, matter is present, and [that whatever comes-to-be is] 'on one hand this, on the other hand that'.

33ᵇ19 Well, then, is there a *sphere* besides [*para*] these [particular spheres], or *house* besides the bricks? Or would there never be any coming-to-be, if it [= form] were a 'this' in that way?* No, [form] signifies a 'such'*, it's not a 'this' and determinate; but rather he makes, or generates°, 'out of this', 'such a thing', and when it has been generated, it's a 'this such'. **ᵇ24** And the whole 'this', Callias, or Socrates, is like the sphere—*this* brazen one, that is—but *man* and *animal* are like *brazen sphere* taken generally.* **ᵇ26** It's evident, therefore, that 'the cause° which consists of the forms' as certain people are wont to call 'the forms' —i.e., if they're things existing besides [*para*] the particulars—, so far as comings-to-be and substances are concerned, is of no use whatever; nor, for the same reasons, can they be substances existing 'in respect of themselves'. **b29** Indeed, it's also evident that in some cases, that which generates is similar [*toiouton*] to that which is generated, not of course the same, or one in number, but one in form, as with the natural [generators and generatees]—for human being generates human being*—unless something comes to be that's 'apart from nature', as 'a horse [generating] a mule' —and these too work similarly; for what would be common to both horse and donkey **34ª**, the nearest genus, doesn't have a name, but it would probably be both, like a mule— **a2** so that it's evident that there is no need to set up a form as *paradigm*—for it was in these cases [= living beings] that [forms] were sought most of all, for these are substances most of all; but that which generates is quite sufficient to the making, and cause of the form being in the matter. **a5** But when once the whole [exists], the form 'such' [*to toionde eidos*] in 'these', flesh and bones, that's Callias, or Socrates; and they are different because of their matter (for that is different); but they are the same in form (for the form is indivisible [*atomon*]).

Zeta 9 [Remarks on "spontaneous" coming-to-be, and on coming-to-be in the nonsubstantial categories. Summary of Z 7-9.]

34ª9 Someone might raise the aporia: why can some things come-to-be both by art and spontaneously, like *health*, while others can't [but only by art], like *house*? The cause is that in some cases the matter—i.e. the matter that initiates the coming-to-be in the making and coming-to-be-something/somewhat that comes 'from' art, and [matter] in

which some part of the product is present—some [matter] is
of a sort to be set in motion by its own agency*, and some is
not, and of the former sort some is capable [of setting itself
in motion] in just the particular way [required], whereas
some is not capable; for many things are capable of 'being
set in motion by their own agency', but not 'in just the particular way [required]' —say, *dancing*. **a16** Things, then,
whose matter is of this sort, e.g. *stones*, can't be set in motion 'in this particular way' [= that requisite for forming a
house] except by the agency of another; yet in another way
they can, too—and so can *fire*. **a18** This is why some things
will not exist without that which has the art [of making
them], whereas other things can; for motion will be started
up by agency of these things that don't have the art, *but are
themselves capable of being moved by *other* things not having the art*, or else 'out of' a part [of the product?].

34ª21 It's clear from what's been said that there's a certain
sense in which all things come-to-be 'out of a homonym'*,
just as do the things [that come-to-be] by nature, or out of a
part that is homonymous (e.g. 'the house out of a house',
qua by the agency of a mind; for the art is the form), or out
of what contains some part,—that is, if it doesn't come-to-be
per accidens; for the primary and 'in respect of itself' cause
of the making [= of its making the product] *is* a part.
a26 For warmth in the motion [= the rubbing] made
warmth in the body; but this either *is* health, or a part of it,
or some part of health follows upon this or health itself does
so; and this is why it's said to 'make' [the health]: it's in the
sense that [the rubbing] 'makes' that upon which [the
health] follows and which it attaches to.

34ª30 So that, just as in syllogisms, substance is the starting-point of all things; for it's from the 'what it is' that
syllogisms start—and it's from there that comings-to-be
[start] too.

34ª33 The case of the 'things that are composited° by
nature'*, too, is similar to these [= the products of art]. For

the seed is productive [lit. "makes"] in the same way as the things from art (for it has the form **34ᵇ** potentially, and that from which the seed is, is in a way homonymous [with the offspring, cf. 34ᵃ22]—for it mustn't be sought that *all* things be like this, [homonymous] in the fashion of 'out of human being, human being'; for also, 'woman, out of man'*— unless it were a case of deformity, which is why 'mule, *not* out of mule'). **ᵇ4** The things which can come-to-be spontaneously, as do those considered above, are those whose matter is capable of being moved by its own agency, with just the same motion that the seed gives it*; but those whose matter is not like this cannot come-to-be in any other way than 'out of those' [= from homonymous parents].

[Appendix to Zeta 7 - 9.]

34ᵇ7 But it is not only with respect to substance that [our] account [*logos*] reveals that the form does not come-to-be; rather, with respect to all primary things the same account applies alike, such as so-much, and so-qualified, and the other categories. **ᵇ10** For just as *the brazen sphere* comes-to-be, but not *sphere* or *bronze*, in the case of *bronze*, too, if it comes-to-be [there's implied a pre-existing matter and form that come to compose *it*]—for always the matter and the form have to exist beforehand; this is also how it is both in the case of the 'what it is', and in that of quality and quantity and the other categories likewise; **ᵇ14** for the quality [*to poion*] doesn't come-to-be, but the qualified wood [*to poion xylon*], nor does the quantity, but the quantified wood or animal. **ᵇ16** But what is unique° about substance, to conclude from these points, is that it is necessary that there exist beforehand another substance, in completedness° [*entelekheiaᵢ*], which makes it, e.g. an animal if an animal comes- to-be; whereas for quality or quantity this is not necessary, rather [these may exist beforehand] only potentially.

Zeta 10 [In what sense does the definition of the 'whole' substance contain the definitions of the 'parts'? When it's the whole substance or form *of* something, and the parts are parts of the form.]

[(1) Must the 'formula' of a substance include the formulae of its parts?]

34ᵇ20 Since [a] the definition is a formula, and [b] every formula has parts, and [c] as the formula is to the thing, so the part of the formula is to the part of the thing,—the aporia already arises: must the formula of the parts be present in the formula of the whole, or not? **ᵇ24** In some cases they [the formulae of the parts] are seen to be present [in that of the whole], but in others [they are] not. The formula of the circle doesn't contain that of the segments, but that of the syllable° does contain that of the phonetic elements°; and yet the circle does divide into its segments just as the syllable [divides] into its phonetic elements.

[(2) Are the parts of a substance 'prior' to the whole?]

34ᵇ28 Then again: suppose the parts are prior to the whole, and the acute angle is part of the right angle, and the finger is part of the man [lit. "of the animal"]; then the acute would [on this showing] be prior to the right angle and the finger to the man. **ᵇ30** But the latter *seem* to be prior; for in formula [the parts] are formulated 'out of' the latter*, and [the wholes] are prior with respect to 'existing without the other', too.*

[(1) again.]

34ᵇ32 Or is "part" being said here in a variety of ways, of which *one* is: "What measures [a thing] in respect of quantity"? —this, let's drop.* But: "Those things 'out of which' the *substance* [is constituted], as *its* parts"? —this, let's investigate.

35ª1 Now, then: if there's matter and there's form and there's what's 'out of' these, and if the matter and the form and what's 'out of' them are substance, then there's [i] a sense in which even the matter is called 'part' of a thing, and [ii] another sense in which it's not, but rather those things 'out of which' the *formula* of the form [is composed] [are called "parts"]. **ª4** For example: [ii] of *concavity*, flesh is not a part (this [= flesh] being the matter* upon which it comes-to-be), but of *snubness* it is a part; then again, [i] of the composite statue, the bronze is a part, but of statue said in the sense of form, it's not—**ª7** for the form, and the thing *qua* having form, is to be called in each case ['the so-and-so', e.g. statue], but the material just in respect of itself is never to be called [that].* **ª9** This is why the formula of the circle doesn't contain that of the segments, but that of the syllable does contain that of the phonetic elements; for the phonetic elements *are* parts of the formula of the form, and aren't matter, whereas the segments are parts in the sense of matter upon which [the form] supervenes—although they're* "nearer" to the form than the bronze is, when roundness is engendered in bronze.* **ª14** But there is a sense in which not even all the phonetic elements will be present in the formula of the syllable, e.g. *these very* [*letters*] *here in the wax*, or *those very* [*movements*] *in the air*; for these *are* already only 'part' of the syllable in the sense of a perceptible matter. **ª17** Indeed if the line, when divided, perishes into the halves, or the man into bones and sinews and flesh, it's not the case that for this reason they [line, man] are [constituted] 'out of these' in the sense of these being parts of the *substance*, but as 'out of' *matter*, and they are parts of the composite, but they are not [parts] of the form, i.e. that which the formula is *of*; **ª21** and for just this reason they are not in the formulae. **ª22** In one sort of case, then, the formula of these sorts of parts will be present, yet in the other, [such a formula] must not be present unless [the whole formula] be [*of*] the whole object taken together [*syneilēmmenon*]°*; for this is why some things arise 'out of' these [parts] as origins [*arkhai*] into which they perish°, while other things don't. ᵃ25 I.e., such things as *are* a form and a matter [lit. "the form and the matter"] taken together, like the *snub* or the *brazen circle*, these things perish into these [materials] and the matter is a part of them; but such things as haven't been taken together [*syneilēptai*] with a matter but are without matter, whose formulae are of the form alone, these things *don't* perish— either they don't at all or not in the same way; ᵃ30 so that these [materials] are origins and parts of the former things [the whole objects, *syneilēmmena*], but are neither parts nor origins of the form. ᵃ31 And this is the reason why the clayen statue perishes into clay, and the brazen* sphere into bronze, and Callias into flesh and bones, *and* the circle into the segments; for there is something which has been incorporated [*syneilēptai*] with the ³⁵ᵇ matter. For *circle* is said homonymously, there's just *circle, simpliciter* [the form], and there's the particular [circle]—on account of there being no name peculiar to the particulars [= particular circles].

[(2) again.]

³⁵ᵇ3 Well, then, the truth has now been stated, but all the same let us say it even *more* lucidly, getting a new grip on the question.

³⁵ᵇ4 Such things as are parts of the formula, into which the formula divides, these are prior—either all or some; but the formula of the right angle doesn't divide into the formula of the acute, rather that of the acute [divides] into that of the right; for the person defining the acute makes use of the right; the acute [being] "smaller than a right angle". ᵇ9 The circle and the semicircle are similarly related; the semicircle is defined by means of the circle, and so is the finger by way of the whole [man], finger [being] "such and such

part of [a] man". **b11** So that such things as are parts in the sense of matter, into which [a thing] divides as into its matter, are posterior; whereas such things as are [parts] in the sense of parts of the formula, and of the substance that's in respect of the formula, are prior, either all or some. **b14** And since the soul of animals (this being the substance of the living thing [lit., "the ensouled"]) is the substance in respect of the formula, i.e. the form, i.e. the Essence of a certain sort of body (at any rate, each part, if the definition is properly done, will not be defined apart from its *work* [= its function], what will not belong to it apart from perception*); **b18** it follows that the parts of this [= soul] are prior, either all or some, to the composite animal, and similarly for each particular [animal], but the body and *its* parts are posterior to this, and what 'divides into these [parts] in the sense of matter' is not the substance [*of* the animal] but the composite. **b22** So these are in one way prior to the composite but in another way not (for [the parts] *can't* even exist separated; for it's not in any old condition the finger of a living thing [lit., "an animal"], but the dead [finger] is a homonym); **b25** but some things are 'simultaneous' [= neither prior nor posterior], the ones that are dominant, and in which the formula and the substance are primarily [lodged], such as, if this be it, *heart*, or *brain*—it makes no difference which of these is of this sort. **b27** But *man* and *horse* and things that apply to the particulars as these do, but 'universally' —these aren't substance, but are a sort of composite of this particular formula and this particular matter, taken universally;* as a particular, though, Socrates *already* consists of ["is 'out of' "] the ultimate matter, and likewise for the other cases.

[(1) again.]

35b31 A *part*, then, can be a part either [a] of the form (by form I mean the essence), or [b] of the composite 'out of' the form and the matter, or [c] of the matter* itself. But only

the parts of the form are parts of the formula, and the formula is of the ³⁶ᵃ universal; for the Essence of circle and
circle, and the Essence of soul and soul, are the same.
ᵃ² But when we get to the composite: e.g. *this* circle, i.e.
one of the particular ones, whether perceptible or
intelligible°—by "intelligible" I mean e.g. mathematical
ones, by "perceptible" e.g. brazen or wooden ones—ᵃ⁵ of
these there is no definition, they are known by thinking or
perceiving, but when they depart from this completedness°
[*entelekheia*] it isn't clear whether they are or are not*;
ᵃ⁷ but they are always formulated/said or known through
the universal formula. But matter, in respect of itself, is
unknowable. ᵃ⁹ Matter can be perceptible or intelligible,
perceptible e.g. bronze and wood and such 'matter' as is
changeable°; intelligible occurring *in* perceptibles not *qua*
perceptible, e.g. the objects of mathematics.

[(2) again.]

³⁶ᵃ¹² It's been stated, then, how matters stand with regard to whole and part, and prior and posterior; and it's
necessary to contend with the question—when someone
asks, "Are *right angle* and *circle* and *animal* prior, or are the
things [prior] into which they divide and 'out of' which they
are, the parts?"—by replying: neither [side is prior] *simpliciter*. ᵃ¹⁶ [i] For if the soul is [identical with] animal or ensouled, or each thing is [identical with] its [soul], and
                circle = Essence of circle,
        right angle = Essence of right angle,
        right angle = the substance of right angle,
then [a] in one way, something [whole] must be called
posterior to something [part], e.g. [posterior] to the things
in the formula and to the [parts of a] particular right angle—
ᵃ²⁰ in fact the [angle] with the matter, the brazen right
angle, and the one in the particular lines [= in 'intelligible
matter'], [are posterior to their parts]—; [b] in another way,

the one without matter is posterior to the things in the formula, but prior to the parts in the particular [instance];—it
mustn't be stated 'simpliciter'. **a24** [ii] But if the soul is different and is not [identical with] animal, even then some
[parts] must be called [prior], and others must not, as has
been said.

Zeta 11 [What things are parts of the form, and what are not parts of the form but of the composite?]*

36ª26 The aporia also reasonably arises, what sorts of
parts belong to the *form*, and what sorts aren't [parts of the
form] but of the [whole thing] taken together*. And indeed
if this isn't clear it's not possible to define any thing; for
"definition's of the universal and the form"; which of the
parts [are parts] in the sense of the matter and which are not,
if *that*'s not apparent, then neither will the formula of the
thing be apparent. **a31** Now, as for things [= forms] that are
found to supervene upon [materials] that are specifically
different, as *circle* does in bronze and stone and wood, it
seems clear for these that neither the bronze nor the stone
belongs at all to the substance of the circle, because it's
separate from them; **a34** but as for the things that are *not*
seen separated, nothing prevents the case from being likewise for **36b** them also, just as even if all the circles that had
ever been seen were of bronze; for no less in that case, the
bronze would still be no [part] of the form; but it would be
hard to abstract it in thought. **b3** For example: the form of
man is always found in flesh and bones and parts of this
kind; are these then parts of the form and the formula? Or
not, but *matter*, but because [man] doesn't supervene on
others [= other matters, types of body] we're unable to
make the separation? **b7** Since this seems to be possible,
only it's not clear *when* [= in what cases], some people raise
the aporia already even in the case of the circle and the

triangle, viz., [saying] "It's not appropriate to define [these] by way of 'lines' or 'the continuous', but rather all these ['lines', etc.] too are [to circle and triangle] in the way that fleshes and bones are to *man*, and bronze and stone are to *statue*"; ᵇ12 they reduce everything to numbers, and say that the formula of *line* is *two*.* And of those who talk ideas, some say that the line-itself [*autogrammē*] is the dyad, others that it's the form of the line, that some things are such that the form and that of which it is the form are the same (e.g. dyad and the form of dyad), but that in the case of *line* this is not so.

36ᵇ17 It then follows both that there's a single form of many things whose form is evidently different (just this conclusion followed for the Pythagoreans also), and it becomes possible to make one thing-by-itself the form of all things, and the others not forms; however in this way all things will be one.

36ᵇ21 That there is some aporia, then, in the business of definitions, and some reason for it, has been stated; and so the reduction of all things [to forms] in this way, and dispensing with matter, is wasted labor; for *some* things, surely, are *this* [*form*] in that [*matter*], or, *these things holding thus*.* ᵇ24 And the comparison, for the case of *animal*, which Socrates the younger used to make*, is not sound, for it leads away from the truth and makes one suppose it a possibility that *man* can exist without the parts, in the way that *circle* can without the bronze. ᵇ28 But it's *not* similar; for an animal *is* something perceptible, and cannot be defined without [reference to] movement, and therefore not without [reference to] '*the parts' holding in some way*'*. ᵇ30 For it's not a hand in just any and every old way that's a part of a man, but one that is capable of fulfilling its work, *ergo*, one that is 'ensouled'; but not ensouled, not a part.

36ᵇ32 But with regard to the mathematika°: why aren't the formulae [of the parts] parts of the formulae [of the

wholes], as the semicircles [are parts] of the circle? For
these aren't perceptible. Or does this [difference between
perceptibles and mathematika] make no difference? For
there will be matter even in some things that aren't perceptible; **37ᵃ** in fact there is some matter in everything that is not
an Essence, I mean [that's not] a form itself by itself, but is
some 'this'. **ᵃ2** These [= the semicircles], then, won't be
[parts] of the universal [circle], but will be parts of the particulars [particular circles], as was said before, for one kind
of matter is perceptible and another kind is intelligible.*

37ᵃ5 It's clear as well that the soul is primary substance,
and the body is matter, and *man* or *animal* is what arises 'out
of' the two, taken universally;* and Socrates and Coriscus,—that is, if [Socrates'] soul is Socrates too—are twofold
(for some take [Socrates] as a soul, others as the composite); **ᵃ9** but if [Socrates and Coriscus are], *simpliciter,
this here soul and this here body*, then as is the universal [the
collective population at large?], so will be the particular.*

37ᵃ10 Whether there is, besides [*para*] the matter of these
sorts of substances, another [kind], and whether it's
necessary to seek some other [sort of] substance, such as
numbers or something like that, must be looked into later
[Books MN?]. For it's the sake of this that we are trying to
determine the [nature of the] perceptible substances also,
since in a certain sense it's the work of physics and second
philosophy, this inquiry about perceptible substances;
ᵃ16 for it's not only about the matter that the physicist has
to know, but also about the [substance] in respect of the formula—and even more so.

37ᵃ18 And in the case of definitions, in what way the
[elements] in the formula are parts [of the definition], and
on account of what the definition is one single formula (for
that the thing is one is clear, but *by what* [*tini*] is the thing
one, in view of its having parts?), must be looked into later
[Zeta 12, Eta 6].

[Summary: Zeta 4-6, 10-11.]*

37ª21 [Zeta 4:] What, then, the Essence is, and in what sense it is 'itself in respect of itself', has been stated generally, for every case; [Zeta 10-11:] and also why the formula of the Essence of *some* things contains the parts of what's defined, but that of *other* things does not, **ª24** and that in the formula of the substance the parts in the sense of matter won't be present—for they aren't parts of *that* substance, but of the composite substance, and of this in a sense there's a formula, and in a sense there's not; **ª27** for of it with its matter there's no formula (for that's in-definite [*a-oriston*]), but with respect to the primary substance, there is one: e.g. of [a] man, there's the formula of the soul; **ª29** for the substance is *the form within* [*to eidos to enon*], 'out of' which and the matter the composite substance is said to be, [Zeta 5:] as is *concavity* (for 'out of' this and *nose* is snub nose and snubness*), but in the composite substance, like a snub nose or Callias, there will also be matter; [Zeta 6:] and that the Essence **37ᵇ** and the thing are in some instances the same, as is the case with the primary substances, e.g. curvature and Essence of curvature, if that's primary (I'm calling *primary* [substance] that which *isn't* said by way of *something being in something else*, i.e. in a subject in the sense of a matter*), **ᵇ4** but those things in the sense of matter or of a compositing with a matter, they're not the same [as their Essences]—nor if they are 'one' per accidens, like Socrates and the musical [one]; for these are the same [only] per accidens.

Zeta 12 [The Unity of Definition (I).]

37ᵇ8 Now let us speak first of definition, to the extent that it has not been discussed in the *Analytics*; for the aporia* that's been spoken of there is applicable to our reasonings about substance. I mean this aporia: that whose formula we

call a definition, why in the world is this *one*?* Take e.g.
man, i.e. *twofooted animal*—let this be its formula.
b13 Why, then, is this one and not many, animal *and* twofooted? For in the case of *man* and *pale* they are many
when the one doesn't belong to the other, but they are one
when it does belong and the subject, the man, suffers°
something (for then a unity comes-to-be, and we have: *the
pale man*); **a18** in our case, however, one doesn't 'share in'
the other—the genus [e.g. animal] doesn't seem to share in
the differentiae° [e.g. twofooted] (for then the same thing
would simultaneously 'share in' contraries—since the differentiae by which the genus is differentiated [lit. 'differs']
are contrary)*. **b21** And even if [the genus] does share in
[them], [we get] the same argument—at least if there is
more than one differentia: e.g. footed–twofooted–featherless. Why are *these* one and not many? Not because
"they're all present [in one thing]"; for that way there'll be
a unity 'out of' everything [that belongs to a thing]. **b24** And
yet—the things in the *definition* have got to be one; for
the definition is a certain *single* formula and *of* [a] *substance*, so that it has got to be the formula of some one thing;
for "substance means some 'one' and some 'this' ", as we
say.

   37b27 We need first to investigate the definitions obtained
by [the method of] Divisions. There is nothing in the definition besides the genus that's said first and the differentiae;
the other genera are the first one; and after it, the combined
differentiae*, e.g. first *animal*, next *animal* [*that's*]
twofooted, and again *animal* [*that's*] *twofooted* [*and*] *featherless*; and similarly **38a** even if it be formulated through further [differentiae].

   38a1 In general it makes no difference whether it's formulated through many or through few—nor therefore
whether through few or through two; of the two one is differentia and the other genus, e.g. of *animal* [*that's*]
twofooted, *animal* is genus and the other is differentia.

38^a5 If, then, the genus absolutely doesn't exist apart from [*para*] the species [*eidē*] as species *of* a genus*, or if it does, then it does as matter (for *voiced sound* [*phōnē*] is genus and matter, but the differentiae make the [various] species, i.e. the [types of] phonetic elements, 'out of' this [= *phōnē*]), then it's plain that the definition is the formula [constructed] 'out of' the differentiae.

38^a9 But actually, in addition the division has to be by the differentiae of the differentia: e.g. a differentia of *animal* is *endowed with feet*; again, the differentia of *animal endowed with feet* has to be *qua* endowed with feet*, **^a12** so that it mustn't be said that of *what's endowed with feet* there's on the one hand feathered and on the other hand featherless, if at any rate he's to formulate properly (rather it's through lack of capacity that he'll do this), but rather there is on one hand [say] cloven-footed and on the other hand not-cloven; for *these* are differentiae of *foot*; for cloven-footedness is a particular [type of] footedness. **^a15** And it wants to proceed always just like this until it gets to the not-further-differen-tiables [*ta adiaphora*]; at that point there will be exactly as many species of *foot* as there are differentiae, and the [types of] *animals endowed with feet* will be equal to the [number of] differentiae. **^a18** If, then, these things stand thus, it's plain that the completing [*teleutaia*] differentia[tion] will be the substance of the thing and the definition, at any rate if it's required *not* to state the same things several times over in the definitions—for that is superfluous. **^a21** But this does indeed occur; for when he says *animal* [*that's*] *endowed with feet* [*and*] *twofooted*, he has said nothing other than *animal having feet having two feet*; and if he divides this by the divi-sion that's proper° [*oikeion*], he'll be saying [the same thing] several times over—as many times as there are differentiae.

38^a25 If then 'a differentia of a differentia' occur [at each stage, as described], the completing one will be single, that is the form [*eidos*] and the substance; but if it were [done] per accidens, e.g. if he divided *endowed with feet* as *pale* and *dark*, then there would be as many of these [differentiae] as cuts. ^a28 So that it's plain that the definition is a formula [composed] 'out of' the differentiae—and it's [out] of the completing one of these, if it's done right. This would be evident if one were to change the order in definitions of this kind—e.g. that of *man*, saying, *animal* [*that's*] *twofooted* [*and*] *endowed with feet*; for *endowed with feet* is superfluous once *twofooted* has been said. ^a33 But there is no 'order' in the substance; for how must we think of one [differentia] prior and another posterior?

^38a34 Concerning definitions obtained by way of Divisions, then, let this much be said as a first [shot], as to what sort they are.

Zeta 13 [Analysis (III). Substance and the Universal.]

^38b1 Since the inquiry is about substance, let· us come back to that. Just as the 'subject' and the Essence and what is 'out of' these are said to be substance, so too is the universal. Now then, two of these have been discussed: the Essence, and the 'subject', [about which we said*] that 'being subject' [or, 'underlying'] is twofold [*hypokeitai dikhōs*], either being some 'this'—as the animal ['is subject'] for the afflictions—or else as the matter ['is subject'] for the completedness [*entelekheia*]; but the universal, too, seems to some to be *par excellence* a [kind of] cause, and the universal to be an origin [*arkhē*] too; hence let us approach this as well.*

^38b8 For it seems impossible that any whatsoever of the 'things said universally' [or: of the things that are called 'universal'] should be substance. ^b9 For [i] first, "substance of each thing is what is co-extensive [*idion*] with each thing, what doesn't belong to something else", but the universal is common [*koinon*], for that is 'said universally' [or: 'called universal'] whose nature is to belong to a number of things.

b12 Then of which will this be substance? Either of all or of none; but 'of all' is impossible—if it is to be of [any] one, then this [one] will be the others too; for "those whose substance is one and whose Essence is one are themselves one". **b15** Then again, [ii] substance means 'what is not [said] of a subject', but the universal *is* said of some subject, always.

38b16 Then could this be right: although [the universal] cannot [be substance] in the way that the Essence is, still it can be *contained in* this [= the Essence], the way *animal* [is contained] in *man* and *horse*? Then clearly there does exist some formula of it. And it makes no difference even if it [= the formula of *animal*] is not the formula of all the things in the substance [= in *man* or *horse*]; for nonetheless this [universal] will be the substance of *something*—as *man* is of the man in whom *it* is present—so that the same result will again follow; for it [= the universal] will be substance of that in which it is present as being co-extensive with it [*idion*].

38b23 But further, it is impossible and absurd that what is 'this' and substance, if it is [composed] 'out of' certain things, should be [composed] not 'out of' substances nor 'out of' what is some 'this', but 'out of' quality; for then non-substance and quality will be prior to substance and what is 'this'. **b27** Just what is impossible; for neither in formula nor in time nor in coming-to-be are the afflictions capable of being prior to the substance; for then they will also be separate [from it].

38b29 Further, in Socrates, a substance will be present, so that it will be a substance of *two*.

38b30 And in general it follows, that if *man* and such things as are said in that way are substance, then none of the things *in* the formula [of *man* and such] is substance of anything nor obtains apart from them [= from *man* and such] nor in anything else, I mean, e.g., there doesn't exist any/some *animal* apart from the particulars [= particular

animals, like *man* and such]*—nor any of the other things
in the formulae.

38ᵇ34 Looked at both on these grounds, then, it is evident
that none of the 'things belonging universally' is substance,
and **39ᵃ** because none of the 'things that are predicated in
common' signifies 'some this' [*tode ti*], but 'such' [*toionde*].
Otherwise, many other [difficulties] result, and the Third
Man.

39ᵃ3 But further, the following is also clear.* Namely, it is
impossible that substance be [composed] 'out of' substances
that are present in it as in completedness [*hōs entelekheiaᵢ*];
for things that are in completedness two in this way are
never in completedness one, though if they are *potentially*
two they can be one (as the double is 'out of' two halves,
only *potentially*, for the completedness [of the halves] sepa-
rates [the double, i.e. destroys it]). **ᵃ7** So that if substance is
one, it can't be [composed] 'out of' substances that are present in it and [present] in this sort of way, which Democritus
correctly formulates; for he says it *is* impossible that there
'come-to-be, out of two, one, or out of one, two' —he's ident-
ifying the substances with his 'atomic magnitudes'.*

39ᵃ11 Moreover, it is clear that it will hold likewise in the
case of number also, at least if number is a 'synthesis° of
units', as is said by some; for either the dyad is not *one*, or
else there is no 'unit', in completedness, within it.

39ᵃ14 But the conclusion contains an aporia. For *if*

    [1] no substance can be [composed] 'out of'
        universals, on the ground that the latter
        signify the 'such' [*to toionde*] but not 'some
        this' [*tode ti*], and *if* also

    [2] no substance admits being composed [*synthe-
        ton*] 'out of' substances existing in completed-
        ness,

then every substance must be incomposite [*asyntheton*], so
that there cannot even be a *formula* of any substance.

39ᵃ19 But surely, it is thought by everyone and was said

long ago* that definition is of substance, if not exclusively,
then most especially.

But now not even of that??

Therefore there can't be definition of anything at all!!

39ª21 Or else 'in one sense there can be, and in another
sense not'.

39ª22 What is being said will be clearer from what is to
come.

Zeta 14 [Platonic ideas are not substance (as the Platonists mistakenly suppose).]

39ª24 It is evident from these very [considerations], also,
what consequence faces those who say that the ideas are
substances existing separately, and at the same time make
the form [species? *eidos*] 'out of' the genus and the differentiae. For if the forms exist, and animal is in man and in
horse, then either it is the same and one in number, or else
it is different; —in formula, clearly it is one; for the formu-
lator [*ho legōn*] will go through the same formula in either
case.*

39ª30 If, then, there is some man, himself in respect of
himself, some 'this' and separated, then necessarily the
things 'out of which' [it (or he) is composed], such as animal
and twofooted, must signify some 'this' and be separate and
be substances; so that animal too [will be like that].

39ª34 Now, if [i] [animal] is the same and one, both the
one in man and in horse, the way you [are the same as and
one] with yourself, then [a] how can the one thing, **39ᵇ** in
the things that exist apart, be one?, why isn't this animal also
apart from itself?* Furthermore, **ᵇ2** [b] if it is to share in
both twofooted and manyfooted, then something impossible
follows, for then the contraries will belong simultaneously
to this thing that is both one and some 'this'; otherwise,
what *is* meant when someone says that animal is twofooted,
or goes on foot? **ᵇ5** But perhaps [the two things, differen-

tia and genus] are "put together", and "in contact", or "mixed"? —but all these are absurd.

39ᵇ7 But suppose [ii] [animal] is different in each. Then there will be, in a word, indefinitely many things whose substance is animal; for it's not per accidens that man is 'out of' animal. **ᵇ9** Further, many [different] things will be animal-itself; for [a] the animal in each [species] will be substance [of that species] (for it is not said 'of something else' [*kat' allo*], and were it otherwise, man would be 'out of' that and that would be its genus*); and further, [b] all the things which man is [composed] 'out of' will be ideas; and so none will be the idea of one thing and substance of another thing (for that is impossible); it follows that each one among the various [species of] animals will be one single animal-itself. **ᵇ14** Further, 'out of' what is *this* [animal for each species] [composed], and how [obtained] 'out of' animal-itself? Or: how can [this] animal, whose substance is exactly this [= animal], exist apart from [*para*] animal-itself?

39ᵇ16 Further, [iii] in the case of perceptible things all these consequences follow and ones even more absurd. If, then, it's impossible for it to be like this, it's clear that there cannot be forms [or ideas] of these [= perceptibles?] in the way that some people say.

Zeta 15 [Individuals do not have definitions (hence neither can Platonic ideas).]

39ᵇ20 Since substance is different, according as what is meant is] [i] the composite and [ii] the formula (I mean, [i] one sense of substance is: the formula taken-together-with the matter*, but [ii] another is: the formula generally),— such things as are called [substances] in the former way, of these there can be destruction° (in fact there can be coming-to-be too), but of the formula there cannot be [destruction] in the sense that *it* ever is being destroyed°—**ᵇ24** for there is no coming-to-be [of the formula] either; for *being house*_d [*to oikia*_i *einai*]* doesn't come-to-be, but only *being this house*_d—but without any coming-to-be or ceasing-to-be they [= substances in the sense of formulae] are, or are not; for it's been shown [Zeta 8] that no one generates these, or makes them. **ᵇ27** For this reason, also of the substances that are perceptible and particular there is neither definition nor proof, because they have matter, whose nature is such that it is capable of both being and not being*; **ᵇ30** which is why all the particulars among them are destructible.

39ᵇ31 If, then, proof is of necessary things, and definition is scientific [*epistēmonikon*] in character, and if, just as it's impossible that knowledge [*epistēmē*] be at one time knowledge and at another time ignorance, but rather it's opinion that's like that, and thus it cannot be proof or definition, but rather it's opinion **40ᵃ** that's *of* what is capable of being otherwise [than it is], then plainly of these [particular perceptibles] there can be neither definition nor proof. **ᵃ2** For they are unclear, the perishing things, to those who have scientific knowledge, as soon as they have passed from perception*, and although the same formulae are preserved*, in the soul, there still will not be either definition nor proof. **ᵃ5** Which is why, when someone sets himself up to make definition* of any one of the particulars, he must be mindful that it can always be confuted; for it's not possible to define [these].

40ᵃ8 Nor is it possible to define any [Platonic] idea. For [i] the idea is a particular, so they say, and separate; and necessarily the formula must be [composed] 'out of' words ["names"], and the definer cannot invent ["make"] a word (for it would be unknown), but the [words] that are to hand are 'common to all'; therefore they must apply [*hyparkhein*] to something other as well; **ᵃ12** e.g. suppose someone were defining *you*, he'll say "*animal* [*that's*] *thin*", or "*pale*", or something else that will apply to another [besides you] as well. **ᵃ14** If someone were to say, "Nothing prevents all

these things separately applying to many, but taken all at
once they apply to this one alone", the reply must be, [a]
first, that they do apply to both of the two [components]—
e.g. *animal that's twofooted* applies to *animal* and to *twofooted* ([a]17 in fact, in the case of eternal things [namely,
ideas], this is even necessary, the [components] being prior
to and parts of the compound [*syntheton*]; more than that,
they are also separate, if man is separate; for either none or
both [are separate]; if, then, nothing [is separate], the genus
won't exist apart from the several species [*para ta eidē*]; but
if it does, then so will the differentia). [a]21 And [the reply
must be] [b] second, that [animal and twofooted] are prior in
their being to [animal that's twofooted], and these aren't
cancelled correspondingly [even if the composite idea,
twofooted animal, be destroyed?].*

40[a]22 Then again, [ii] if the ideas are composed 'out of'
ideas (for the things 'out of which' are less compounded than
the composite), it will yet further become necessary that
these *components* of the idea be predicated of a plurality [of
subjects]—for example, animal and twofooted must be; if
not, how will they get to be known?*; for then there will be
a certain idea which it is impossible to predicate of more
[subjects] than one. But *that* doesn't seem to be the case,
rather every idea [supposedly] is sharable-in [*pasa idea
einai methektē*].

40[a]27 Well then, as has been said [[a]17 ff. above], it
escapes notice that definition is impossible in the case
[even] of eternal things [if they are particulars], especially
such as are unique, like Sun or Moon. For they go wrong not
only in attaching things such that even were they removed,
the Sun would still exist, like "revolving round the Earth",
or "hidden at night" (for [if such were part of the "definition" of Sun, then] if it stood still, or shone [at night], the
Sun would no longer exist— but that's absurd, if it had to
stop [existing, under these circumstances]; for *the Sun*
means a certain *substance*); but further, [they also go wrong

in attaching] things that can apply to another subject, e.g. if
a second thing of this sort comes to be, clearly it will be a
Sun; **40ᵇ** therefore the formula is common; but now, wasn't
the Sun a particular, like Cleon and Socrates?

40ᵇ2 Why is it that none of these people produces a definition of an idea? It would become plain if they tried, that
what has just been said is true.

Zeta 16 [Neither the parts of substances, nor the basic elements, are substances.]

40ᵇ5 It's evident that even of the things supposed to be
substances, most are [really] potentialities: both the parts of
animals (for none of them can exist having-been-separated,
and when they *are* separated, then they 'are', all, [only] in
the sense of matter) and earth and fire and air; for none of
them is *one*, but they're like a heap°, until they're worked
up* and some kind of unity* comes-to-be 'out of' them.
ᵇ10 Especially one might suppose that the parts of the living
things [lit. "the ensouleds"] and the parts of the soul respectively corresponding most closely to them, would come-to-
be both [substances and potentialities], since they are both
in completedness and potentially [even at the level of
'parts'], because of having origins of movement from
something in their joints; which is why some animals can
live when divided. **ᵇ14** But all the same, the [parts] all will
'be' [only] potentially*, when they are [fused into] *one*
[organism] and are continuous by nature—but not by force,
or by [an abnormal] growing-together*; for that sort of
thing is a deformity.

40ᵇ16 Since *one* is said like *being*, and the substance *of*
what's one is one, and things whose [substance] is one in
number are one in number, it's evident that neither one nor
being is capable of being substance *of* things*, just as
neither Essence of element [*being an element*d] nor Essence
of origin [*being an origin*d] could be; but we seek what,

then, the origin is—so that we may 'reduce to what is more
knowable' [Zeta 3 *fin.*]. [b]21 Now indeed, of these, being
and one are more substance than are origin and element and
cause, but still even these are not at all [substance], at least
if "nothing else that's common is substance"; for "substance belongs to nothing but itself and what has it, of which
it is the substance". [b]25 Again, what's *one* can't be in many
places at once, but what's *common* does occur at many
places; so that clearly none of the universal things occurs
apart from the particulars [*para ta kath' hekasta*], separately. But those who speak of the forms in one way speak
rightly, that they're separate, *if* they're substances, that is,
but in another way wrongly, in that they say the 'One-over-
Many' is a form. [b]30 The reason is that they don't know
how to render which things are the substances of this sort—
the indestructible ones apart from the particular and perceptible ones—so they make these the same in form as the
destructible ones (for the latter are the ones we know), man-
itself and horse-itself, attaching to the perceptibles the tag
[*rhēma*] "itself". And yet, even if we had never [41a] seen the
stars, nonetheless, I imagine, they would still have *been*
eternal substances besides the ones we knew; so that now,
too, if we can't say which ones these are, all the same
perhaps it's necessary that some such do exist.

[41a]3 Well, then, that none of the things said universally
is substance, and that no substance is 'out of' substances,
is clear.

Zeta 17 [Analysis (IV). A "new beginning": Substance as Form.]

[41a]6 What, and what sort of thing, substance should be
said to be, let us formulate this again, making as it were
another beginning; for perhaps from this we may also get
clear about that substance which exists separated from the
perceptible substances.*

41ᵃ9 Since, then, substance is a certain principle and cause, let us pursue it from that point. **ᵃ10** Now, the *why* [*to dia ti*] is always sought in this form: *why does one thing belong to something else?* For to inquire why the musical man is a musical man is either to inquire what was just said, namely why the man is musical, or something else. **ᵃ14** Now *why a thing is itself* [or why X is X, or why XY is XY] is no question at all. For the 'that', the obtaining of the *belongs*-relation, must be clear—I mean, *that* the Moon is eclipsed; but *that* a thing is itself [or that X is X] is a single formula or a single 'cause' applying to *all* cases; "Why's the man a man?" and "Why's the musical [thing] musical?"*— unless one were to say, "because each thing is indivisible from itself and that *is* [its] *being one*₍d₎"; but that's common to everything and an easy way out [lit. a "shortcut"].

41ᵃ20 But if one inquire, *why such-and-such a kind of animal is a man?**, then this much is plain, one is *not* asking *why he who's a man is a man**. **ᵃ23** Therefore the question is: given *something of something* [*ti kata tinos*], *why* does it belong? *That* it belongs has to be plain; if it doesn't [isn't?], there's *no* question. [So] it's like [the question]

why does it thunder?

[equalling the question]

why does noise occur in the clouds?

41ᵃ25 In this way [= thrown into this form] the object of inquiry *is* [after all] *something of something else* [*allo kat' allou*].* And [similarly]: Why are *these*, bricks and stones, say, a *house*? So it's evident that the cause is being inquired after, [and that's the Essence, as we say *logikōs*;]* which in some cases is, For what purpose? ["for-the-sake-of-what?"]°, as perhaps e.g. for *house*, or *bed*; in other cases it is, What first set the movement going?, for that's a cause too. But while the latter sort of cause is sought in the case of coming-to-be and passing-away, the former [can be sought] in the case of being also.

41ᵃ32 The thing being inquired after escapes notice most of all in those cases where things aren't [explicitly] *said of* one another, **41ᵇ** as e.g. when it is asked *what man is*, because it's said *simpliciter* ["impacted", *haplōs*], and it isn't separated out, that *these* are *this*. **ᵇ3** But before we inquire it needs to be articulated out; if it isn't, then it's all one whether we're inquiring into something or nothing. **ᵇ4** But since the being [*einai*] must hold ["belong"] and be assured, clearly the question is *why the matter is some definite thing* [*ti*]*;

e.g.:   [Q:] Why are these things a house?

        [A:] Because there belongs what it is to be [a] house$_d$.

        [Q:] Why is this—or [better], this *body*, thus-and-so conditioned [*to sōma touto todi ekhon*], a man?

41ᵇ7 So the cause is being sought (and this is the form) of the matter's being some [definite] thing [*ti*]; and this is the substance. **ᵇ9** It's plain, then, that in the case of the simple [= impacted, cf. ᵇ1 above] terms, the inquiry or instruction can't get going, but rather a different type of inquiry is [requisite] for such things.*

41ᵇ11 Since* what is compounded 'out of' something in such a way that the whole is *one*, not like a heap but like the *syllable*—**ᵇ12** but the syllable is not its elements, $\beta\alpha$ is not the same as β and α,* nor is *flesh* fire and earth (for when they have been sundered, the wholes, e.g. the flesh and the syllable, no longer exist, but the elements [of the syllable] exist, and so do the fire and the earth; **ᵇ16** therefore, the syllable is something, not just the elements, the sounded [= a vowel, α] and the unsounded [= a consonant, β] but also something else, and the flesh is not just fire and earth, or hot and cold, but also something else—**ᵇ19** and if, then, that further thing itself has to be either an element or composed 'out of' elements, then [a] if it's an element, the same argument will apply again—for the flesh will be made of this [further thing] + fire + earth, and something else *again* [will be needed]*, and so on indefinitely. **b22** [b] And if it's made 'out of' an element, clearly it won't be 'out of' one but more than one, or else [if of only one] that one will be the thing itself, so that again we can make for this case the same argument as for the flesh, and the syllable. **b25** It would seem rather that this further thing is something and is *not* an element, and is the *cause* of *this-being-flesh*, and *that-being-a-syllable*; and likewise for the other cases. **b27** And this is the substance *of* each thing, the primary cause of its being; but while some things aren't substances, still such substances as there are, are composited* in accordance with a nature and by way of a nature of their own, **b30** and that very nature would appear to be [their] substance, and that's *not* an element, but a *principle* [*arkhē*], **b31** an 'element' being that into which a thing can be divided, being present in it as matter, like the α and the β of the syllable.

H

Eta 1 [Review of the project. Perceptible substance and matter.]

42ª3 We must reckon up the results out of what has been said, and drawing together the main points, add the completion°. It has been said [Zeta 1] that the inquiry is into the causes and the origins and the elements of substances. [Zeta 2] And some substances are agreed upon by all, whereas of others, certain people have been advocates from their own standpoint. "Agreed upon" are the natural ones, such as fire, earth, water, air and the rest of the 'simple bodies', and then the plants, and their parts, and the animals, and the parts of animals, and finally the universe [lit. "heaven"] and the parts of the universe; but some people say from their own standpoint that the forms and the mathematika are substances. **ª12** [Zeta 3, 4] But from arguments it follows that substances are other than these, namely the Essence and the Subject [are substances]; in a different way again, [that] genus is more [substance] than the species [pl.], and the universal more than the particulars; **ª15** [Zeta 14] and with the universal and the genus are connected the ideas (for it's by the same argument that they are supposed to be substances). **ª17** [Zeta 4, 6] And since the Essence is substance, and formula of the essence is the definition, for this reason there has been discussion of definition and of the 'in respect of itself'; [Zeta 10-12] and since the definition is a formula, and the formula has parts, it was necessary also to see concerning *'part'* what sorts of things are parts of substance and what are not, and whether these are parts of the definition too. [a]21 [Zeta 13, 16] Further, too, neither the universal nor the genus is substance; as for the ideas and the mathematika, this will be looked into later; for some people say that these are substances, besides [*para*] the perceptible substances.*

[42a]24 But now, let us return to the substances that are agreed upon. These are the perceptible ones, and all perceptible substances have matter. Now the subject is substance, and in one sense this is the matter (I mean by matter that which, though it is not some 'this' actually°, is potentially some 'this'), but in a second sense [the subject] is the formula and the shape, which being some 'this' is separate in formula*; and thirdly, what is 'out of' these, of which alone there is coming-to-be and ceasing-to-be, and which is separate *simpliciter*; for of 'substances in respect of the formula', some are [separate] and some are not*.

[42a]32 But that matter also is substance is clear; for in all changes° [*metabolais*] between opposites there is something that is subject for the changes, e.g.

> [a]34 with respect to place, there's that which is now here and now elsewhere, and
> [a]35 with respect to growth, there's that which is now of one size and then again smaller or larger, and
> [a]36 with respect to alteration, there's that which is now healthy [42b] and then again ill;

similarly also with respect to substance, there's that which is now in process of coming-to-be and then again in process of passing-away, and [there's that which] now is subject in the sense of some 'this', and then again is subject in the sense of 'with respect to a lack'.*

[42b]3 And the other changes are entailed by this one, but this one isn't [necessarily] entailed by either one or both of the others; for it's not necessary, if something has matter for [change of] place, that it also have matter for being generated or passing-away.*

42ᵇ7 What the difference is between coming-to-be *simpliciter*, and not *simpliciter*, has been stated in the writings on nature.*

Eta 2 [The Analysis of Substantial Being.]*

[1. 1042ᵇ9-24 Manyness of differentia: some pseudo-substantial analogies.]

42ᵇ9 Since the substance [that serves] as 'underlying' [*hypokeimenon*], i.e. as matter, is generally agreed upon, and this is the one that exists potentially, it remains to say of the substance as *actuality* of perceptible things, what it is.

42ᵇ11 Now Democritus, for his part, seemed to be of the opinion that there are *three* differentiae [entering into the constitution of things]—for the body that underlies—the matter—is one and the same, but it 'differs',

either [a] by way of 'rhythm'—i.e. configuration [*skhema*],

or [b] by 'turning'—i.e. position [*thesis*],

or [c] by 'mutual contact'—i.e. order [*taxis*].

42ᵇ15 Evidently, though, there are *many* differentiae, e.g.

ᵇ16 [i] some things are constituted [lit., "are said"—are *defined*?] by a *composition* [*synthesis*] of the matter, such as things that are constituted ["said"] by *blending*, like honeywater,

ᵇ17 [ii] others by *tying*, like a bundle,

[iii] others by *gluing*, like a book,

ᵇ18 [iv] others by *nailing*, like a box,

[v] others by more than one of these,

ᵇ19 [vi] others by *position*, like a threshold or a lintel—for these 'differ' by being placed thus-and-so,

ᵇ20 [vii] others by *time*, like dinner and breakfast,

ᵇ21 [viii] others by *location*, like the winds,

[ix] others by the afflictions [proper] to
      perceptible things, like hardness and
      softness, and density and rarity, and dry-
      ness and wetness, and
[a] [of these], some by some of these
      [afflictions],
[b] others by them all,
      and in general, some by excess, some by
      defect.

[2. 1042^{b}25-28 False start on the analysis.]

^{42b}25 Therefore, it's clear that the *is* [of substantial be-
ing], too, 'is said' in exactly as many ways* [as the aforesaid
manyness of differentia]: a threshold *is*, in that it-lies thus*,
and the '*being*' [*to einai*] means [*sēmainei*] *its lying thus*,
and *there being ice* [means] *being solidified thus**.

[3. 1042^{b}28-1043^{a}4 Manyness of differentia: gesture at some better cases.]

^{42b}28 Of some things the 'being' will even be defined by
all of these [marks], by some [parts'] being mixed, some
blended, some bound, some solidified, and some employing
the other differentiae, as do *hand*, and *foot*.
^{42b}32 The *kinds of differentiae* [*ta genē tōn diaphorōn*],
then, must be grasped, for these differentiae are going to be
principles of [substantial] being [*arkhai tou einai*]; for example, the things [differentiated] by the 'more and less', or
by 'dense and rare', and by the others of this sort; for all
these are [forms of] *excess and defect*. ^{b}35 And if something
is [differentiated] by way of shape, or by smoothness and
roughness, all these are [differentiations] by [forms of]
straight and curved. And for still other things, ^{43a} 'being'
will be *being-mixed*, and 'notbeing' the opposite. —^{a}2 It's
evident, then, from these [forms of differentia], that if in

fact the substance is the cause of each thing's being, it's in them that it's got to be sought what the cause of each of these things' being is.

[4. 1043^a4-7 Disavowal of the examples.]

^{43a4} Now *in fact*, none of these* is really [an instance of] substance, [neither in themselves] nor 'coupled' [= with a matter], but all the same that which is *analogon* [to each other, and to real substantial 'being'] is in each of them; and as among substances what gets predicated of the matter is the actuality itself, [so] among the other definitions too [sc. in our examples], [it should be what] most of all [corresponds to actuality].*

[5. 1043^a7-12 Statement of the analysis.]

^{43a7} For instance: if we had to define *threshold*, we'd say *wood or stone lying like THIS*, or *house*: *bricks and boards lying like THIS*—or again, the purpose [*hou heneka*] would go in too in some cases; and *ice*: *water frozen or solidified like THIS*; or *harmony*: *THIS sort of mixture of high and low*; and similarly in the other cases.

[6. 1043^b12-28 Consolidation and conclusion.]

^{43a12} It's evident, then, from these [cases? considerations?] that the actuality of one matter is different from that of another*, and [so is] the formula; for of some things it's the composition, of others it's the mixing, and of others it's some other of the ones we've mentioned. **^{a14}** This is why, of those who give definitions, the ones who, saying *what a house is*, [say] that [it is] *stones and bricks and timbers*, are speaking of the-house-potentially, for those are [the] matter; but those who proffer *a receptacle that shelters chattels and bodies*, or something else of that nature, are speaking of the actuality; but those who combine both of these [speak of] the third [kind of] substance, the one [composed] 'out of' the first two; **ª19** for it seems that the formula that is given through the differentiae is of the form and the actuality, whereas that which is 'out of' the components is rather of the matter—and similarly for the sorts of definitions that Archytas used to accept; for they are of both-combined.

43ª22 E.g.: *What is still weather?* Absence of motion in a large volume of air; the air is matter, the absence of motion is the actuality and substance. *What is a calm?* Smoothness of sea; the subject in the sense of matter is the sea; the actuality and the shape is the smoothness.

43ª26 It's evident, then, from what has been said, what perceptible substance is, and how it is: there is substance as matter, and again as shape and actuality, and third the kind that is composed 'out of' these.

Eta 3   [Composite and form; form and number.]*

43ª29 It must be borne in mind that sometimes it's hard to tell ["escapes notice"] whether the name signifies the compound substance or the actuality and shape*—e.g. *house*, whether it's a sign of the common thing, because it's *a covering of bricks and stones laid THUS*, or [it's a sign of] the actuality and form, because it's *a covering*; and *line*, whether it's *a two in length* [= dimension?], or *a two*; and *animal*, whether it's *a soul in a body*, or *a soul*—for a soul is actuality and substance of some body. **ª36** *Animal* could even apply to both of these, not in the sense of [both of these] being formulated [defined?] in a single formula, but as 'referred to one thing' [*pros hen*]*. But although these things make a difference with respect to another purpose, with respect to the inquiry about **43ᵇ** perceptible substance they make none [= make no difference]; for the Essence belongs to the form and the actuality. **ª2** In that soul and Essence of soul [being a soul_d] are the same, but Essence of man and man are not the same, unless the soul too is to be called man; so "in one way yes, and in another way no".*

43ᵇ4 Now, it's apparent to those who investigate that the syllable is not 'out of' the phonetic elements *and* their composition, nor is the house bricks *and* composition. And this is right—neither the composition nor the mixing is among [= is one of]* the things they are composition or mixing *of*. **ᵇ8** Likewise not in any of the other cases either, e.g. if the threshold [is such] by position, the position isn't composed 'out of' the threshold but more like vice versa, threshold 'out of' position.* **ᵇ10** Nor indeed is the man animal *and* two-footed, rather there has to be something besides these, if these are [= were] matter, [something else] which is [= would be] neither an element, nor composed 'out of' elements, but substance; but leaving this out, they formulate [only] the matter. **ᵇ13** If, then, this is [the] cause of the [thing's] being and this [or: the cause] is substance, they can't be formulating the substance itself.

43ᵇ14 This [= substance], then, either must be eternal, or it must be destructible without its ever being the case that *it* is being destroyed, and must have come-to-be without its ever being the case that it is coming-to-be*. But it's been proved and made clear elsewhere [Zeta 8] that no one makes or generates the form, instead a 'this' is made, and the '[composite] "out of" these' comes-to-be. **ᵇ18** Whether the substances *of* destructible things [can] exist separately, is [up to now] most unclear; except it's clearly impossible in some cases, cases where the things can't exist apart from their individual specimens, e.g. *house*, or *tool*. **ᵇ21** Indeed, maybe they aren't even substances, neither these things themselves nor any of the others that aren't composited by nature*; for one might hold that the nature [in natural objects] is the *only* substance to be found among destructible things.

43ᵇ23 Therefore the puzzle [*aporia*] that the Antistheneans and like ignoramuses used to puzzle over has a certain timeliness, viz.: "it's impossible to define the 'what it is' " —for "definition is a 'long harangue' "—but 'what sort of thing it is' it is actually possible to explain; e.g. *silver*, not what it is, but that it is like tin; [b28] so that of one kind of substance there can be definition and formula, e.g. of the composite kind, whether it's perceptible or whether it's intelligible; [b30] but the primary things 'out of' which this is [composed] cannot in turn be defined, that is, if the formula—the definitory one—signifies 'something of something' [*ti kata tinos*], and the one must play the role of matter and the other of form.

[43b32] It's apparent as well, if substances are in some way *numbers*, why they are so in this way and not, as some allege, by being numbers of 'units'; for the definition is a sort of number; for it is divisible, and indeed into indivisibles—for the formulae aren't infinite—, and number is like that. [b36] And just as when one of the parts 'out of' which a number is composed is subtracted from or added to the number, it's no longer the same number but a different one, even if the very least part [44a] is subtracted or added, so neither the definition nor the Essence will exist any longer if anything is subtracted or added. [a2] And the number must be something in virtue of which it is one, but now they can't say 'by what' it is one—at any rate if it's one (for either it's not, but like a heap, or else if it is, then it must be stated what it is that *makes* it one 'out of' many); and the definition is one, and in the same way they aren't able to say what makes *it* one, either. [a6] And this is a plausible result; for the argument is the same, and the substance is one in the manner we have indicated, not as some allege, by being a sort of "unit" or "point"; but each [substance] is a completedness [*entelekheia*] and a kind of nature. [a9] And just as the number doesn't have a 'more' or a 'less', neither does the substance in respect of the form—rather, if at all, it's that which involves matter.*

[44a11] Concerning the coming-to-be and passing-away of what are called substances, then, how it's possible and how

not, and concerning the reduction to number—let this suffice for an account.

Eta 4 [Levels of matter. Clarification of subjecthood of 'afflictions'.]

44ª15 About material substance: mustn't forget that even if all things are 'out of' the same *primary* [material] or [out of] the same things as *primary* [elements], and if the same matter serves as origin [*arkhē*] for the [various] things that come-to-be, all the same there is a certain proper [matter] of each; **ª18** as of *phlegm*, it is the sweets and the fats, but of *bile*, it's the bitter or some other things—but it may be that these all [ultimately] are 'out of' the same [primary, original matter(s)]. **ª20** There come to be several matters of the same thing, when one [matter] is matter of another, as *phlegm* is 'out of' fat *and* sweet if the fat is 'out of' the sweet, and [something] is 'out of' bile by decomposing into its primary matter, the bile*. **ª23** For "*this* 'out of' *that*" is twofold, there is [a] "*this* will be, further along the way", and [b] "[*this* will be, when *that*] is decomposed into its original [matter] [*eis tēn arkhēn*]". **ª25** It can happen that various different things come-to-be although the matter is one, because of [difference in] the moving cause, as 'out of' wood, both box and bed. **ª27** But of some things, since they are different, their matter is of necessity different, as a saw couldn't be 'out of' wood; this isn't in the power of the moving cause, for it can't make a saw 'out of' wool or wood. **ª29** But if the same thing can be made 'out of' a different matter, then it's clear that the art, and the origin in the sense of moving, must be the same; for if both the matter *and* the mover are different, then the product [= thing that has come to be, *to gegonos*] must be also.

44ª32 When, then, someone seeks the cause, since the *causes* are said in several ways, it's necessary to state all the possible causes. For example:

What's the cause of a man in the sense of matter?
   The catamenia?
What is it in the sense of mover?
   The seed?
What is it in the sense of the form?
   The Essence.
What is it in the sense of "for the sake of which"?
   The **44ᵇ** completion.

Perhaps these last two are the same. It is the *nearest* causes that must be stated. "What's the matter?" [should be answered with] not *fire*, or *earth*, but the matter that's peculiar to the thing [*tēn idion (sc. hylēn)*].*

44ᵇ3 Regarding the substances that are natural and come-to-be, then, it's necessary to pursue them in this way if one is to pursue rightly, and one needs to recognize the causes—*if*, that is, the causes are these and this many; but for the substances that are natural and eternal, another account [is needed]. For it may be that some [of these] don't have matter, or not [matter] of this kind but only for movement with respect to place.

44ᵇ8 As for such things as *are* by nature, but are *not* substances: there is *not* matter for these; but rather, the 'subject' is: *the substance*. For example:

   What's the cause of an eclipse? What's its matter?
     There isn't any; what undergoes the affliction is: *the Moon*.*
   What's the cause in the sense of moving and extin-guishing the light?
     The earth.
   Probably there's no 'for the sake of which' [in this case].

The cause in the sense of form is the formula; but this is unclear unless the formula includes the [moving] cause. For example [trying again on the 'form' of eclipse]:

   What is eclipse?

Deprivation [lack, *sterēsis*] of light.

But if "by the earth's coming in between" had been added, *that's* the formula that includes the cause.*

44ᵇ15 In the case of *sleep*, it's not clear what is the primary thing that undergoes the affliction. Is it the animal? Yes, but the animal with respect to what, what primarily? The heart? Something else? **ᵇ18** Then, 'by the agency of what'? Then, 'what' *is* the affliction? Is it of this [primary subject], and not of the whole animal? Is it *an absence of movement, of THIS kind*? Yes, but this is by way of the primary [subject's] undergoing *what*?

Eta 5 [Brief sketch of substantial change by de-differentiation.]

44ᵇ21 Since some things are, and are not, without any coming-into-being and passing-away*, like *points*, if indeed they 'are', and generally the forms too (for the white$_n$ doesn't come-to-be, but rather the wood [comes-to-be] white$_a$, if every thing that comes-to-be 'comes-to-be out of something' and 'comes-to-be something' [Z 7 init. etc.]), not all contraries could come-to-be 'out of' each other, but it's in different senses that 'a pale$_a$ man out of a dark$_a$ man' and 'pale$_n$ out of dark$_n$'; **ᵇ27** nor is there a matter of everything, but only of such things of which there is coming-to-be and change into each other; but such things as are, or are not, without [such] changing, there is no matter of these.

44ᵇ29 There's an aporia how the matter, the matter of each thing, stands with reference to contraries. For example, if the body is potentially healthy, and contrary to health is illness, then is [the body] potentially *both*? And is the water potentially [*both*] wine and vinegar? **ᵇ32** Or is it [= body, water] 'matter of' one in respect of a possession° [*hexis*] and in respect of form, and of the other in respect of a lack and a corruption that is contrary to its nature?* **ᵇ34** It's a parti-

cular aporia too why the wine is neither matter of the
vinegar nor potentially vinegar (after all, vinegar does
come-to-be 'out of' it), nor the living being potentially a
dead body. No: rather, **45ᵃ** [these] corruptions are per accidens, it's the *matter* of the animal that is itself by way of *its*
corruption a potentiality or matter for a dead body, likewise
the *water* [not the wine, that's matter] for vinegar; for they
come-to-be 'out of' these [vinegar from wine, corpse from
animal] in the fashion that night [comes-to-be] 'out of' day.
ᵃ3 And such things as 'change into one another' in this way
must go back to their matter—e.g., if 'out of' a dead body
[there came to be] an animal, it must first [go back] to the
matter, then in this way [= 'out of' the matter] an animal;
and the vinegar to water, then in this way [= 'out of' the
matter] wine.

Eta 6 [The Unity of Definition (II).]

45ᵃ7 About the aporia stated earlier, concerning *definitions* and concerning *numbers*: what's the cause of their unity? [lit., "their being one?"]*. For of all things having a
number of parts, and where the totality isn't like a *heap*, but
the whole is something besides [*para*] the parts, there's
some cause; since even among bodies*, in some cases *contact* is cause of their unity, in other cases *stickiness*, or some
other such affliction. **ᵃ12** Now a definition is one formula
not by a bond [or]* in the fashion of the Iliad, but by being
of one thing [*henos*]*. **ᵃ14** Well, then, what is it that makes
man one? Why one and not many, like both animal *and*
twofooted—especially, indeed, if there are, as some say, a
particular animal-itself and twofooted-itself? Why aren't
those-themselves man, and the men will 'be' by participation, not in *man*, not in one, but in two, animal *and* twofooted, and generally man wouldn't be one but more than
one, animal and twofooted?

45ª20 Plainly then for those who pursue defining and formulating as they are accustomed, it's not possible to answer and solve the aporia; **ª23** but if, as *we* formulate it, there is on the one hand matter and on the other form, and the one potentially and the other actually, then the topic of investigation would no longer seem an aporia. **ª25** For this aporia is the same even if the definition of *cloak* were: *rounded bronze*; for then this name would be a sign [= abbreviation?] of the formula, so that the topic of investigation is: what's cause of the unity of the rounded and the bronze. But then it's clear there's no aporia any longer, because 'the one [aspect] is matter, the other is form'. **ª30** Then what's cause of *this*, namely of what is potentially [something] *being* actually [so], aside from the maker, in the case of things where there is genesis? For there is no other cause of what is potentially sphere being actually sphere, but this [= the cause] was the Essence for whichever of the two it is.*
ª33 Of *matter*, there is intelligible *and* there is perceptible, and always of a formula one [aspect] is a matter and another is an actuality, like *circle = plane figure*. **ª36** But such things as don't have matter either intelligible or perceptible, each of these is straight off **45ᵇ** 'just what is some one' [*hoper hen ti*], just as it's also 'just what is some being' [*hoper on ti*]—the 'this', the so-qualified, the so-much—which is also why neither "being" nor "one" is present in their definitions—and the Essence is straight off 'some one', just as it is also 'some being'—which is why there is no *other* thing that's cause for any of *them* being 'one', nor of their being some being either; **ᵇ5** for each of them is straight off 'some being' and 'some one', not in the sense of being in the genus 'being' or 'one', nor in the sense of their being separate, apart from [*para*] the particulars.

45ᵇ7 It is because of this very aporia that some people speak of "participation" [*methexis*], and puzzle over [*aporousin*] what's the cause of participation and what

participating is; and others again [speak of] "communion"
[*synousia*]*, in the sense that Lycophron says "knowledge
[is a 'communion'] of knowing and soul", and others say that
"life [*to zēn*] is a 'composition' or a 'connection' of soul to
body". **ᵃ12** And yet the same account applies to all cases;
for in fact *being healthy* [*to hygiainein*] will be either a
"communion" or "connection" or "composition" of soul
and health, and *the bronze being a triangle* will be a "composition" of bronze and triangle, and *being pale* a "composition" of surface and pallor. **ᵇ16** The reason is that they seek
a unifying [lit., *henopoion*, "making-one"] formula and differentia of potentiality and completedness. **ᵇ17** But, as has
been said, the final matter and the shape are the same and
one, [the one] potentially, the other actually, so that investigating What's the cause of unity and of being one*, is similar; **ᵇ20** for each thing is 'some one', and what is 'potentially' and 'actually' are after a fashion one, so that there is no
other cause—besides that, if any, which brought about the
movement from potentiality to actuality. **ᵇ23** And such
things as have no matter, are all *simpliciter* 'just what is
some one'.

Θ

Theta 1* [Potentiality "in the strict sense": to produce "movement".]

45ᵇ27 That which primarily is, and to which all the other categories of that which is are referred, has been discussed —that is, substance; for it is with respect to the formula of substance that the others are said to be, the quantified and the qualified and the others that are said in this way; for they all will contain the formula of substance, as we said in the earliest discourses [= Zeta 1]. **ᵇ32** And since that which is is in one way said by being *what* or *something** and qualified and quantified, but in another way with respect to potentiality and completedness, and with respect to function, let us now make determination concerning potentiality and completedness; and first concerning potentiality in its strictest sense, even though it is not the sense that is most useful for **46ᵃ** what we are now after; for potentiality and actuality are said in more cases than those regarding movement alone. **ᵃ2** But when we have talked about that sense [= in chs. 1-5], we shall then, in the determinations of actuality [= in chs. 6-10], shed light on the others also.

46ᵃ4 Now then, that potentiality [*hē dynamis*] and being potential [*to dynasthai*] are said in many ways, has been determined by us elsewhere [= Delta 12]; of these, on one hand, those that are called potentialities homonymously* may be left aside (**ᵃ7** for some are said by a [mere] resemblance, as in geometry we say that things are or are not "powers" [*dynata*] by way of being or not being such-and-such); on the other hand, [the potentialities that are said] with reference to the same form are all origins [*arkhai*] of some kind, and are said with reference to one primary [potentiality], namely, *origin of change* [*arkhē metabolēs*] *in another or* [*in itself*] *qua other*. [a11] For one kind is a potentiality of being acted upon, the origin, in the the thing itself that is acted upon, of being affectively changed by agency of another or of [itself] *qua* other; [a13] whereas another kind is a tendency of not being affected for the worse nor of being destroyed by agency of another or [of itself] *qua* other by agency of an origin of change. [a15] Present in all these definitions is the formula of potentiality in the primary sense. Again, these potentialities are said [to be] either of acting or being acted-upon alone, or of [acting or being acted-upon] *well*, so that even in the formulae of the latter, the formulae of the prior potentialities are in some way contained.

[46a19] It's plain, then, that in one way there is a single potentiality of acting and being acted-upon (for [something is] potential both by itself having the potentiality of being acted-upon and by another thing [having the potentiality of being acted-upon] by agency of it), but in another way they are different. [a22] For one is in that which is acted-upon (for it's because it has a certain origin, and because even the matter is a kind of origin, that what is acted-upon is acted-upon, [one thing by agency of one,] another by agency of another; for the oily is burnable, and what yields in *this* way is crushable, and likewise in the other cases); [a26] but the other [potentiality] is in that which acts, e.g. heat and house-building [art], one in that which heats, the other in that which house-builds; which is why, insofar as naturally constituted*, nothing is acted-upon by agency of itself; for it's *one*, and not 'other'. [a29] And incapability [*adynamia*] and the incapable [*adynaton*] are the lack that is contrary to this sort of potentiality, so that every potentiality is *of* the same thing and with respect to the same thing as a [corresponding] incapability. [a31] Lack is said in many ways; for there is

[1] 'that which [simply] doesn't possess', and [2] 'that which is naturally suited [to possess], *but* doesn't possess', either [a] at all, or [b] when it is naturally suited [to possess], and either [i] in *this* way, as [when it doesn't possess] completely, or [ii] not at all. ᵃ34 And in some cases, where things naturally suited to possess, fail to possess by force, we say they 'are lacking'° [*esterēsthai*]*.

Theta 2 [Rational and nonrational potentiality.]

46ᵃ36 Since some of these sorts of origin are found in inanimate things, and others in animate things, and in soul, and in 46ᵇ the part of the soul that has reason [*logos*], it is clear that some potentialities will be non-rational and some rational [*meta logou*]; which is why all the arts and productive knowledges are potentialities; for they are origins of change in another or *qua* [an]other.

46ᵇ4 And for all of the rational [potentialities], the same [potentialities] are of their contraries, but for the non-rational, one [is only] of one; e.g. the hot only of heating, but the medical art of both illness and health. ᵇ7 The reason is that knowledge is a formula, and the same formula reveals both the thing [*to pragma*] and its lack, only not in the same way, and in a sense it's [formula] of both, but in a sense it's more of that which belongs [than of the lack or of the 'thing lacking']; ᵇ10 thus it's necessary that these sorts of knowledges also be of their contraries, but of the one [contrary] in respect of themselves* and of the other not in respect of themselves*; ᵇ12 for the formula is of the one in respect of itself, and of the other, in a sense, per accidens; for it's by negation and removal that it reveals the contrary; for the contrary is the primary lack, and this is the removal of the other [= the positive thing]. ᵇ15 But since contraries don't occur in the same thing, but knowledge is a potentiality by having a formula, and the soul has an origin of movement, [it follows that] whereas the healthful produces only health, and what heats, heat, and what chills, coldness, the knower [can produce] both [contrary effects]. **ᵇ20** For the formula is of both, though not in the same way, and it's in a soul which has an origin of movement; so that [the soul] will move both from the same origin, having linked them up with reference to the same thing [= the same formula]; which is why the things that are potential with respect to a formula produce contraries*; for they are encompassed by a single origin, the formula.

46ᵇ24 It's plain also that the potentiality of merely doing or being-done-to is implied in the potentiality of [doing or being-done-to] *well*, but not always vice versa; for necessarily, he who does well also does; but it's not necessary that he who only does also does well.

Theta 3 [Potentiality defended against Megarian criticism.]

46ᵇ29 There are some who say, such as the Megarians, that a thing is capable [of acting] only when it *is* acting, but when it's not acting it's not capable [of acting]*, e.g. he who isn't house-building, isn't capable of house-building, but only he who is house-building, when he is house-building; and likewise in the other cases.

46ᵇ32 That the consequences of this are absurd, it's not hard to see. [1] For it's clear that he won't even be a house-builder unless he is house-building (for to be a house-builder *is* to be able [*dynatos*] to house-build), and likewise with the other arts. **ᵇ36** Now, if it's impossible to have such arts without at some time having learnt and acquired them, and [impossible then] to not-have them **47ª** without having at some time lost them (that is, either by forgetting or by some affliction or by time; for the *subject-matter* doesn't pass away, it's always there), when he's stopped, he won't have the art! but he'll straightway start house-building again, how'd he get it back? **ª4** And inanimate things are the same

way: there won't be cold or hot or sweet or anything perceptible at all unless perceivers are [actually] perceiving them;
so that they'll have to maintain the doctrine of Protagoras.
ᵃ7 But indeed, neither will anything have perception if it is
not perceiving, i.e. acting [*energei*]. So if 'blind' is 'not having sight, being naturally constituted [to have it] both when
so constituted and still being so', then the same people will
be blind many times per day; deaf, too.

47ᵃ10 [2] Again, if that which is lacking in a capability is
incapable [*adynaton*], then that which is not happening will
be incapable of happening; yet he who says of what is incapable of happening either that it is or that it will be, will
speak falsely (for incapable *meant* this); therefore these
theories [*logoi*] do away with both movement and coming-
to-be. ᵃ15 For what stands will always stand, and what sits
[always] sit; for it won't get up, seeing as it's sitting; for what
can't [*mē dynatai*] get up, is incapable of getting up. ᵃ17 So
if we can't say this, it's evident that potentiality and actuality are different (but those theories make potentiality and
actuality the same, so it's no small thing they seek to do
away with), so that it's possible that something be capable of
being [*dynaton ti einai*] and yet not-be, or capable of not-
being and yet be, and likewise for the other things-
predicated: being capable of walking, not-walk; walk,
though being capable of not-walking. ᵃ24 And *this thing is
capable* [or possible, *dynaton*] *if there will be nothing impossible* [*adynaton*] *in its attaining the actuality of which it's
said to have the capability* [or possibility, *dynamis*]*. ᵃ26 I
mean, e.g., if [a thing] is capable of sitting and it's open to
it to sit, then if [in the future] sitting should [actually]
belong to it, there will be nothing impossible [in this]; and
likewise if it is [capable of] being moved or moving, or of
standing or causing to stand, or of being or coming-to-be, or
of not being or not coming-to-be.

47ᵃ30 That which is named 'actuality' [*energeia*], which is
connected to 'completedness' [*entelekheia*]*, has been extended [lit., "has proceeded"], from chiefly [applying to]

the movements, to other things too; for it seems that actuality is especially [or "in the strictest sense"] movement; which is why they don't assign movement [*to kineisthai*] to things that are not, although certain other predicates they do, e.g. things that are not are objects of thought or of desire, but things-moved they aren't, and this because though they *aren't*, in actuality [and thus can't be moved?], they *are going to be*, in actuality [and thus can be thought and desired?]. **47ᵇ** For of things that are not, some are, potentially; but [still] they *are* not, because they are not in completedness.

Theta 4 [Potentiality as possibility.]

47ᵇ3 If what has been described is the possible [*dynaton*] [Theta 3 47ᵃ24-26] or is compatible with it*, evidently it cannot be true to say that *this here is possible* [*dynaton*], *but will not be*, which would have the consequence that the things that cannot be [*ta adynata einai*] would on this showing vanish*; I mean, e.g., suppose that someone were to say, that it's *possible* that the diagonal be measured*, but nonetheless it *will not* be measured—someone, that is, who isn't considering [*mē logizomenos*] that it's incapable [*adynaton*] of being—, on the ground that nothing prevents something being capable of being or of coming to be from neither being nor going to be. **ᵇ9** But from the assumptions the following is necessary: that if we were to suppose that which is not, but is capable [of being], to be or to have come to be, nothing impossible [*adynaton*] will be; but [here] an impossible *will* result, for [the diagonal] being measured is impossible. **ᵇ12** For the false and the impossible are *not* the same; that you are standing now is false, but not impossible.

47ᵇ14 At the same time it is also clear that if, when A is, B must be, then, if A is possible, B must be possible*; for if B need not be possible, then nothing prevents its not being possible. **ᵇ17** Now, let A be possible. **ᵇ18** Then, when A was possible, [47ᵃ24-26] if A was posited [to be], nothing

impossible followed; and then B must of course be [possible]
also. ^b20 But [B] was supposed impossible. Then, let it be
impossible. Now, if B is impossible, then A must be so also.
^b21 But the first [= B?] *was* [supposed] impossible; there-
fore the second [= A?] must be impossible too. ^b22 If, then,
A is possible, then B will also be possible, on the assumption
that they were so related that if A is, then B must be. ^b24 If,
then, A and B being so related, B be not possible on this condition ["if A is possible"], then A and B will not be related
as was supposed ["A is implying B is"]; and if, if A is possible, B must be possible, then, if A is, B must also be.
^b27 For 'that B must be possible, if A is possible', *means* the
following, 'that if A *is*, both when and in the way that [it was
supposed] capable of *being*, then it's necessary that B then
and in that way *be* also'.

Theta 5 [How capabilities (*dynameis*)
are acquired and exercised.]

^{47b}31 All capabilities being either innate, like the senses,
or [acquired] by practice, like the [capability] of flute-play-
ing, or [acquired] by learning, like the [capability] of the
arts—[we] must possess those acquired by practice and by
reason [*logos*] having previously exercised [*pro-energēsan-
tas*], but for those [= innate] not of this sort and those having to do with passivity this is not needed.

^{47b}35 Since that which is capable ^{48a} is capable of some-
thing and at some time and in some way and all the other
things that must be present in the determination, and [since]
some things are capable of producing movement [*dynatai
kinein*] by way of reason and their capabilities involve such
reason, whereas other things are non-rational and their
capabilities are non-rational, and the former [capability]
must be in a living thing, whereas the latter can be in both
[living and non-living];—with the latter sorts of capability,
when the active and the affectible come together as 'being
capable' [*hōs dynantai*], the one must act, the other must be

acted on; but with the former sort [= the rational] this is not necessary; for all these [non-rational capacities] are 'one [capability] productive of one [thing]', but those [= rational] [are productive] of contrary effects, so that [if they produced them automatically or necessarily] they will produce [both] contraries simultaneously; but this is impossible [*adynaton*]. [a10] There must therefore be something else that's in charge [*heteron ti to kyrion*]; I mean, desire or choice. [a11] For whichever of two things [the animal] desires overridingly, this it will do when it's present [*hyparkhei*] and comes together with the affectible as 'being capable'; so that everything that's 'capable by way of reason', when it desires that for which it has the capability and in the way [circumstances?] in which it has it, must do this; and it has [the capability] when the affectible is present [*parontos*] and thus-and-so disposed [*hōdi ekhontos*]; otherwise, it won't be able [*ou dynēsetai*] to act. ([a16] It serves no further purpose to add the determinative condition, 'nothing external preventing'; for [the animal] has the capability in the sense that it's a capability for acting, and this is not under all circumstances but under certain conditions ["things-being-*so*"], among which will be the exclusion of external hindrances; for these are precluded by some of the conditions present in the determination [of the capability].) [a21] Hence, even if one has a wish or a desire to do two things or contrary things at the same time, one won't do them; for it's not in *that* way that one has the capability of them, nor is it a capability for doing both at once, since one will do those things of which [it's a capability], in the way in which [it's the capability of them].

Theta 6 [*Energeia/dynamis* distinction distinguished from *kinēsis/dynamis* distinction.]

[48a25] Since potentiality with respect to movement has been discussed [chs. 1-5], let us now determine of actuality, both what actuality is, and what kind of thing. In fact the

potential too will at the same time become clear as our analysis proceeds, in that we do not call potential only that whose nature is to move [*kinein*] another, or to be moved by agency of another, either *simpliciter* or in some particular way, but also in the other sense; and it is on account of this [other sense of potentiality] that in the course of our inquiry we have discussed these [cases of potentiality for movement] as well.

48ª30 In fact, actuality is the belonging of the thing [*to hyparkhein to pragma*], not in the manner we call 'potentially'; we speak of 'potentially', e.g.,

> 'a Hermes in the wood', and
> 'the half-line in the whole,

i.e., it could be separated out, and [we call] 'knowledgeable' even him who is not theorizing, if he's capable [*dynatos*] of theorizing. On the other hand, [there is the manner we call] 'actually'.

48ª35 What we mean to say will be clear from the particular cases by induction; and one must not look for a definition of every thing, but must survey the analogy: that

> as what is house-building **48ᵇ** is to what can build, and
> as what is awake is to what is asleep, and
> as what is seeing is to what has its eyes shut but has sight, and
> as what has been shaped out of the matter is to the matter, and
> as the wrought is to the unwrought—

of this difference let one member be defined as the actuality, the other as the potential. **ᵇ6** 'Actually' is not said in every case in the same way, but by analogy: '*as* this is in this or in reference to this, *so* that is in that or in reference to that'. **ᵇ8** *In some cases* [= *actuality*] *is as movement in relation to potentiality; in other cases it is as substance in relation to some particular matter.*

48ᵇ9 But also the infinite and the void, and things like that, are said [to *be*] potentially and actually, in another way

than many [other] things-that-are, e.g. than that which sees
or walks or is seen. ^b12 For the latter things can even
sometimes be truly predicated *simpliciter* (for the seen
["visible"] [is so called] on one hand because it's being seen,
or on the other because it's capable [*dynaton*] of being seen);
but the infinite is not potentially in this sense, that it's going
to be actually independent [*khōriston*], but it is [separate]
for knowledge. ^b15 For the dividing never coming to an end
yields the result that *this* actuality exists potentially, but not
that [the infinite] exists separately [*khōrizesthai*].

48^b18 Since among actions that have a limit [*peras*], none
is a completion [*telos*], but each is the sort of thing *relating
to* the completion,—as e.g. slimming is to slimness; the
[bodily parts] themselves, when they are slimming, in that
respect are in movement, though those things which the
movement is for the sake of [whose presence constitutes
slimness] do not yet belong to them—these things are not action, or at least not complete, just because it is not a completion. ^b22 But that [sort of action] in which its completion is
contained is a [real] action. ^b23 E.g., in the same moment
one is seeing and has seen [= "knows" by sight], is understanding and has understood [= possesses understanding],
is thinking and has thought [= "knows" by insight].* But if
you are learning, it's not the case that in the same moment
you have learned, nor if you are being cured, that in the
same moment you have been cured.* ^b25 However, someone who is living well, at the same time has lived well, and
someone who is prospering, has prospered. If that were not
so, [the living well, e.g.] would have had to come to an end
at some time, as is the case with slimming [= when the state
of slimness, of one's having completed an act of slimming,
has been achieved]. But in fact it does not; you are living and
have lived. ^b28 Of these [actions], then, one group should
be* called *movements*, and the other, *actualizations*. For
every movement is incomplete—slimming, learning, walking [= walk-taking], house-building; these are movements

and are incomplete. **ᵇ30** For one cannot in the same moment both be taking a walk and have taken it, nor be house-
building and have house-built, nor be coming-to-be and
have come-to-be, nor be being moved [*kineitai*] and have
been moved [*kekinetai*]; they're different, as [in general] are
moving [*kinei*] and having moved [*kekineken*]*. **ᵇ33** But at
the same moment the same thing has seen and is seeing, and
is thinking and has thought. This sort of thing, then, I call an
actualization, the other sort, a movement.*

48ᵇ35 What is actually, then, what it is and what sort of
thing, may be regarded as clear from these and like cases.

Theta 7 [When is X potentially Y?]

48ᵇ37 But when each thing *is* potentially, and when not,
must be determined—**49ᵃ** for it's not [potentially] at just any
time whatsoever. For example, is *earth* potentially *a man*?
Or not, but rather when it's already become semen, and
perhaps not even then?* **ᵃ3** It's just like the way not everything can be *made-healthy*, whether by medical art or by
luck, but there's a certain thing that's capable [*dynaton*] [of
that], and that's what's healthy potentially. **ᵃ5** And definitory of what comes-to-be in completedness from *thought* out
of what is potentially, is that when it is willed [by the agent]
it comes about as long as nothing external hinders; on the
other side, in what's being healed, when none of the things
in *it* hinders. **ᵃ8** It's in the same way that a house too is
potentially: if none of the things in this, i.e. in the matter,
hinder its coming-to-be a house, and if there's nothing that
has to be added, or taken away, or changed, then this is
potentially a house; and it's like this for the other things the
origin of whose coming-to-be is *from without*.

49ᵃ13 Whereas for things where [the origin] is in the thing
itself that has it, [it is potentially] all such things as will be
through it [or "of its own power", *di' autou**] if nothing from
without trips it up; e.g. the semen is not yet [potentially

a man] (for it needs to be cast into another, and to change-
over [*metaballein*]*); but when through its own origin it *is*
already in this state, then it's already potentially *this* [= a
man]; but the former is in need of another origin, just as
earth is not yet potentially a statue—for it's got to change-
over [*metabalousa*], and it will [first] be *bronze*.

49ª18 It seems that what we call not "*this*" but "*that-
en*"*—e.g.

> the box is not *wood* but *wooden*, and
> the *wood* is not *earth* but *earthen*,

and once again if *earth* is likewise not another [*that*] but
thaten—[it seems, then, that] always the *that* is, put *simpliciter*, potentially the adjacent thing up in the sequence.
ª22 For example, *the box* is not *earthen*, nor [of course]
earth, but is *wooden*; this [= some wood] is what's potentially a box and this is matter of a box, i.e. *wood simpliciter*
of *box simpliciter*, and of this box, this wood. **ª24** But if
there's something primary, which is not yet called "*thaten*"
with respect to another thing ["*that*"], then this is a prime
matter; e.g.: if

> *earth* is [not *air* but] *air-y*, then
> *air* is not *fire* but *fiery*, and
> *fire* is prime matter, since it is not an individual
> "this" [*tode ti*].*

49ª27 For, *the "that of which"* [*to kath' hou**], or *the "subject"* [*to hypokeimenon*], are differentiated in the following
way: [i] by being an individual "this", or else [ii] not being
one. **ª29** For example, [i] the "subject" for the *afflictions* is:
a *man*, i.e. a body and soul; while the affliction is musical,
or pale (the thing is called, when the music comes to be in
it, not music but music*al*, and the man not pallor but *pale*,
and not a walk or a movement but walk*ing* or mov*ing*—just
as with "that*en*")—well, then, whenever it's like this, the
ultimate [subject] is: *a substance*; but [ii] whenever it's *not*
like this, but what's predicated is a particular form and a
particular "this" [*eidos ti kai tode ti*], then the ultimate

[subject] is matter, substance in the sense of a matter. ^a36 So it turns out to be the right result that ^49b "thaten" is said with respect to both the matter and the afflictions; for they're both [in contrast to the substance] in-definite [*a-orista*].

^49b2 Well, then, it's now been stated when a thing should be said to be potentially, and when not.

Theta 8 [Actuality prior to potentiality.]

^49b4 Since it's [been] determined in how many ways the *prior* is said [cf. Delta 11], it's evident that actuality is prior to potentiality. I mean by potentiality not only that definite kind which is called 'origin of change in another or [in itself] *qua* other' [Theta 1 46^{a}11, etc.], but quite generally, every origin, movemental or static. ^b8 For *nature* is in the same genus as potentiality; for it's a movemental origin, only not in another, but in [the thing] itself *qua* itself.—To all this sort of [potentiality], then, actuality is prior, both [1] in formula, and [3] in substance; but [2] in time, [it's prior] in one sense, but in another not.

^49b12[1] Well then, that it's prior in formula, is clear; for what's potential in the primary sense is potential because it admits becoming active [*energēsai*], e.g. I mean by 'capable of house-building' [*oikodomikon*] that which can house-build [*to dynamenon oikodomein*], and by 'capable of seeing' [*horatikon*] [that which can] see [*to (dynamenon) horan*], and by 'visible' [*horaton*] that which can be seen [*to dynaton horasthai*]; and the same formula applies to the other cases too, so that the formula and the knowledge [of the one] must precede the [formula and] knowledge [of the other].

^49b17 [2] In time, [a] it is prior in the following sense: that which is active [*to energoun*], which is identical in species, though not in number, is prior [= to the potential cospecific thing it can produce]. ^b19 I mean this, that [b] to this individual man already existing in actuality [*kat' energeian*], and to the wheat and to [the animal] seeing, the matter and the seed and the capable-of-seeing [*horatikon*], which are potentially man and wheat and seer, but not yet actually, are prior in time; however, [a] prior in time to these are other things which *are* actually, from which these came-to-be. **b24** For always out of that which is potentially, that which is actually comes-to-be, by agency of that which is actually, e.g. man out of man, musician by agency of musician, always when some thing is moving first; and the mover already is actually. **b27** It was said in the writings about Substance [see Zeta 7] that everything that comes to be, comes to be out of something, [comes to be] something, and by agency of something, and this last the same in species.

49b29 This is also why it is thought impossible [*adynaton*] for one who has house-built nothing to be a house-builder, or for one who has never harp-played to be a harpist; for he who's learning to harp-play, learns to harp-play harp-playing, and the others likewise. **b33** Whence arose the sophistical elenchus that the one who doesn't have the knowledge will be doing that which the knowledge is [knowledge] of*; for the one who's learning does not have it. **b35** But [in answer to that], because, of that which is coming-to-be, something has [must have] come-to-be, and generally of that which is changing [*kinoumenou*], something has [must have] changed [*kekinēsthai*] (this is made clear in the work on Movement [*Physics* vi 6]), **50a** he who is learning, too, necessarily has something of the knowledge, it seems. **a2** But then, in this too it's clear that actuality is also in this sense prior to potentiality, i.e. in respect of coming-to-be and time.

50a4 [3] However, [actuality is also prior] in its very substance, first [a] because the things that are posterior in coming-to-be are prior in form and in substance (such as male adult [prior] to boy and human being to seed; for the one already *has* the form and the other doesn't), and because everything that comes-to-be goes [lit., "walks"] toward a first principle [*arkhē*] and a completion (for the for-the-sake-of-which [of something] is a first principle, and the coming-to-be is for the sake of the completion), and the actualization is the completion, and it is for the sake of this that the potentiality is acquired. [a10] For it's not that animals see in order that they may have sight, rather they have sight so that they may see, and likewise [they have] house-building art so that they may house-build, and the theoretical [capacity] so that they may theorize; but they don't theorize so that they may have theoretical [capacity], except those who are practising, and these don't theorize except in this particular sense, or because they don't need to theorize*. [a15] Furthermore, the matter *is* potentially, because it may go into the form; and when it *is* actually, then it is in the form. [a16] And it's the same way in the other cases, including those in which the completion is a movement, which is why just as teachers think that once they have exhibited [the pupil] actually at work [*energounta*], they have delivered the completion, nature as well does likewise. [a19] For if it does not come about in this way, it will be the Hermes of Pauson*; for it's not clear whether the knowledge is within or without, just as with him [= the Hermes]. [a21] For the work [*ergon*] is a completion, and the actuality is the work, hence even the *name*, "*en-ergeia*", is said with respect to the *ergon*, and aims at [contributes to?] the completedness [*entelekheia*].

[50a23] And while in some cases the exercise [*hē khrēsis*] is the final thing (e.g. for sight, the seeing, and nothing else besides this comes-to-be from sight), in other cases something does come-to-be (e.g. from the house-building, a house, besides the house-building), all the same, [the exercise] is in the former case no less the completion, and in the latter case more completion than is the potentiality; for [the act of] house-building is [realized] in that which is being house-built, and comes-to-be, and is, at the same time as the house.

50ª30 In the cases, then, where what comes-to-be is something different, apart from the exercise, in those cases the actualization is in what is being made [the *poioumenon*] (e.g. the [act of] house-building is in that which is being house-built, and the [act of] weaving in that which is being woven, and likewise also in the other cases, and in general the movement in the thing that's being moved [the *kinoumenon*]); but in the cases where there's not some other work [*ergon*] apart from [*para*] the actualization [*en-ergeia*], the actualization is present in them [= the agents] (e.g., the seeing in the seer and the theory in the theorizer and the **50ᵇ** life in the soul, and hence the well-being too; for that's a certain sort of life).

50ᵇ2 So that [summing up 3(a)] it's evident that the substance and the form are actuality. Indeed, according to this argument it's evident that actuality is prior to potentiality in substance, and as we have said [in (2), 49ᵇ17-29], in time one actuality always precedes another, one before another until the [actuality] of that which firstly and always causes movement.

50ᵇ6 But then, [b] [actuality is prior] in a stricter sense also; for eternal things are prior in substance to perishable things, and nothing potentially *is* eternal. **ᵇ8** Here is the reason: every potentiality is at the same time [a potentiality] of the contradictory; for whereas that which is not capable [*dynaton*] of belonging can't belong to anything, yet everything that is potential [*dynaton*] still admits of not being actual [*mē energein*]. Therefore, *being capable* [*dynaton*] admits both [actually] being, and [actually] not being; therefore, the same thing is capable of both being and not being. **ᵇ12** And that which is capable of not being, admits of not being; and that which admits of not being is perishable, either *simpliciter*, or in just that sense in which 'to admit of not being' is said, whether with respect to place or quantity or quality [or whatever]— '*simpliciter*' meaning 'with respect to substance'. **ᵇ16** None of the things, there-

fore, that are 'imperishable' *simpliciter* are 'potentially'
simpliciter (though nothing prevents this 'in a certain
respect', e.g. [being potentially] so-qualified or placed);
b18 therefore they all are actually; nor can any of the things
[be potentially] that *are* of necessity (**b19** you see, these are
primary; for if these were not, nothing could be); **b20** nor, if
there is any eternal movement, can it [be potentially]; nor,
if there is any eternal thing-moved [*kinoumenon*], can it be
moved by way of a potentiality, except of 'whither-whence'
(for nothing prevents a matter of this from being present),
hence [the] sun and stars and the whole heaven are always
active [*aei energei*], and there is no fear lest they sometime
may stop, which is what those who [study] 'about nature'
fear.* **b24** Nor doing this do they tire; for the movement is
not for them connected with the potentiality of the opposite,
as it is for perishables, so that the continuity of the movement would be toilsome; for it's the fact that substance is
matter and potentiality, [it's] not actuality, that's cause of
this.

50b28 The imperishables are also imitated by the beings
that are involved in change, like earth and fire. For these too
are always active [*aei energei*]; for they have their movement both of themselves [*kath' hauta*] and in themselves [*en
hautois*]. **b30** But the other potentialities, from the determinations that have been made [50^{b}8-12 above], are all of the
opposite—for that which is capable [*dynamenon*] of moving
[something] *thus* can also [move it] *not thus*—that is if [they
are] according to reason [*kata logon*]; and the same non-
rational [potentialities] by their belonging or not will be
[potentialities] of the [thing or the] opposite.

50b34 If, therefore, there are any natures or substances of
the sort that they speak of who discuss the ideas, there must
be something much more knowing than knowledge-itself
51a and [more] mobile [*kinoumenon*] than movement; for
these are more actualities, and those [knowledge- and
motion-themselves] are potentialities for these.

51ª2 That actuality, then, is prior both to potentiality and to every origin of change, is evident.

Theta 9 [Various remarks on potentiality and actuality.]

51ª4 That the actuality is also better and more valuable than the good potentiality, is clear from the following considerations. For such things as are said with respect to 'being capable' [*dynasthai*], the same is capable [*dynaton*] of contraries, e.g. that which is said to be capable of being healthy, the same is capable of being ill, and [it's capable] of both at once; for it's the same capability for being healthy and sick, and for resting and moving, and house-building and tearing down, and house-being-built and falling down. **ª10** The being-capable of contraries, then, is present at the same time; but the contraries at the same time is impossible [*adynaton*], and the actualities belonging at the same time is also impossible, e.g. being healthy and sick, so that necessarily the good is one or other of these, but the being-capable is of both alike, or neither; therefore the actuality is better. **ª15** Necessarily also in the case of bad things, the completion and the actuality are *worse* than the capability; for the same thing is 'capable' of both contraries alike. **ª17** It's clear therefore that there is no bad apart from the [bad] things; for the bad is by its nature posterior to the capability. **ª19** Therefore, in the things that are from the beginning and eternal, there is nothing either bad or failed or destroyed—for destruction is a bad.

51ª21 The geometrical constructions [diagrammata, lit., "lines through"] are found out actually; for they find them when they divide. If the divisions had [already] been made, they would have been obvious; but as it is they are present potentially. Why is the triangle two right angles? Because the angles around one point are equal to two right angles. If, then, the [line] had [already] been drawn up parallel to the side, the 'why' would have been immediately plain to whoever looked. [a27] The angle in a semicircle universally a right angle, why? If three lines are equal, the two that compose the base and the perpendicular from the center, it's plain to whoever looks who knows the former [proposition]. [a29] So it's evident that things that are potentially are found out when they are drawn into actuality; the reason is that the actuality is thinking; so that the potentiality [proceeds] out of actuality, and it is by this means that in making [the diagrammata] people come to know [them]—although the individual actuality is posterior in its generation [to] the corresponding [potentiality].

Theta 10 [Truth.]

[51a34] Since *what is* and *what is not* are said, [a] with respect to the schemata of the categories, [b] with respect to the potentiality or actuality [51b] of these or their contraries [incapability, non-actuality], [c] of true and false; and [since] this last is, as regards the objects, through their being combined or separated, so that he has truth who thinks the separated to be separated and the combined to be combined, and he has falsehood whose thought holds contrarily to the objects—[all this being so], when is there, and when is there not, what's called truth and falsehood? [b6] For it must be examined what we mean [by these]. For it's not because of our truly thinking you to be pale that you are pale, but because of your being pale that we who say this have the truth. [b9] If, then, some things are always combined and impossible [*adynata*] to have been separated, and some things are always separated and impossible to have been combined, whereas others admit of [*endekhetai*] the contraries [of being separated and being combined], then *being* is being combined and being one, and *not-being* [is] being not-combined but more than one; regarding the 'admitters' [*endekhomena*], then, the same opinion and the same statement

comes-to-be false and true, and *it* 'admits of' at one time
having truth, and at another time having falsehood; but
regarding the things that are incapable [*adynata*] of holding
otherwise, it doesn't come-to-be at one time true and at
another time false, but the same things are always true, or
always false.

51ᵇ17 But now regarding the non-composites [*asyntheta*],
what is being or not-being, and the true and the false? For
it's not compound, so as to 'be' when it is put together, and
to 'not be' if it is separated, in the way of 'the wood [being]
white', or 'the diagonal [being] incommensurate'; nor will
the true and the false still be present in like fashion to the
former cases. **ᵇ22** Rather, just as the true is not the same in
these cases, in the same way neither is being; instead, [1]
the one thing is true or false [as follows]: contact and saying
are truth (saying [*phanai*] not being the same as affirming
[*kataphanai*]), but ignorance is not-touching. **ᵇ25** For it is
not possible to be in error concerning *what it* [= *a thing*] *is*,
except per accidens; and likewise concerning the non-composite substances, for it's impossible to be in error [about
them either]; and they all are actually, not potentially, for
[otherwise] they'd have come-to-be and passed away, but as
it is, being itself neither comes-to-be nor passes away, for [if
it did] it would have to have come-to-be out of something.
ᵇ30 As for those things, then, that are just what is some being [*hoper einai ti*] and actualities, about them it's not possible to be in error, but only to either think* them or not. But
their *what it is* is inquired into, i.e., whether they are such-
and-such, or not.

51ᵇ33 [2] As for the being corresponding to the true, and
the not-being corresponding to the false, there's one case
where, if they're put together, there's truth, and if they're
not put together, there's falsehood; and there's the other
case, where if the thing *is*, it *is thus*, **52ᵃ** but if it is not thus,
it is not; and the true is to think these things, and there is no
falsehood, nor error, but ignorance, only not like blindness,

for blindness is as if someone altogether lacked the thinking faculty.

[52a4] It's evident also that about the immovables [*akinēta*], error is not possible with respect to time, if one supposes them immovable. E.g. if it's thought that the triangle does not change, then it won't be thought that at one time it 'has two right angles' but at another time not (for it would have to change); [but it can happen that] 'a particular one [is], a particular one [is] not', e.g. [it may be thought, wrongly, that] no even number is prime, or [alternatively, rightly, that] 'some are, some are not'. [a9] But about a number that's *one* in number, not even this [sort of error can occur]; for no longer will it be thought that 'a particular one [is], a particular one [is] not', but what's held will be truth or falsehood, as its eternally obtaining thus.

I

Iota 1　[Unity.]

52ª15 That *one* [or *that which is one*, or a *unit**] is said in many ways, has been mentioned earlier in our remarks 'on the number of ways' [in which things are said] [i.e., Delta 6]; but while it is said in more ways [than the following], there are four main 'modes' of the things that are primary* and called *one* in respect of themselves, and not per accidens.

52ª19 [1] That [is one] which is continuous, either *simpliciter*, or especially that which [is continuous] by nature, and not by contact or by tying (and of these, that is *more* 'one' and prior, whose movement is more indivisible and more simple);

52ª22 [2] Even more of this sort [= continuous*?] is that which is a whole, and has a certain shape and form; and especially if something is of this sort [= is a whole having a certain shape and form?] by nature, and not by force, as are such things as are [wholes etc.] by gluing or nailing or tying-together*, but has in itself the cause of itself being continuous. **ª25** It is of this sort [= as described] because its movement is one and indivisible in place and time; so that it is evident that if something has by nature an origin [*arkhē*] of movement—the primary origin (I mean, e.g. circular locomotion), of the primary movement (I mean, e.g. locomotion), then this is the primary 'one' [or 'unit'] magnitude.

52ª29 Some things, then, are one in this way, by being continuous or whole; other things [that are one] are those whose formula is one, and such are the things of which the thinking is one, and such [in turn] are the things the [formula or thinking] of which is indivisible, but it's indivisible when the thing is indivisible either [4] in form or [3] in number.

52ª31[3] 'In number', then, the particular is indivisible;

52ª32[4] 'in form', that [which is indivisible] in intelligibility [*gnōstō*i] and in understanding [*epistēmē*i], so that that would be a *primary* 'one' which was cause of the substances' being one.

52ª34 *One*, then, is said in this many ways: [1] the continuous by nature and [2] the whole, and [3] the particular [= one in number], and [4] the universal [= one in form], and all these are one because of the indivisibility of either 52ᵇ the movement in some cases, or of the thinking or the formula in the others.

52ᵇ1 But it is necessary to understand that [the questions], 'what sorts of things are called a unit?' and '*what is it to be a unit* [= what is essence of unit] and what is the formula of it?' should not be taken as equivalent. ᵇ3 For 'a unit'* is said in this many ways, and each thing [X] to which one of these modes [of being one] belongs will be a 'unit'; but *to be a unit* [= essence of unit] sometimes will be to be [= essence of] some one of these [X], and other times to be something else that's even closer to the name, whereas the former things [are closer] to the power [i.e., the things the name names]*—ᵇ7 just as it is also with 'element' and with 'cause', if one had to explain both the things to which they apply and the definition [*horon*] of the name. ᵇ9 (For in one way fire is an element (or perhaps it is the *apeiron* or something else like that [that is an element] in respect of itself), but in another way not; ᵇ11 for *to be fire*d and *to be an element*d are not the same, for although as a particular thing and a nature fire is an element, still the name ["element"] means that the following is a property of it: that *something is 'out of' this as primary constituent.* ᵇ14 And it

is thus also with 'cause' and 'one' and all things like these.)
^{b}15 And this is why *to be a unit$_d$* [= the essence of unit]* is
to be indivisible$_d$, [*to be*] *being$_d$ HOPER this and separate$_d$,
on its own$_d$*, either in place or in form or in thought, or
again, [*to be*] *whole$_d$ and indivisible$_d$*, but most of all, *to be
the first measure$_d$ of each genus*, and above all, of [the
genus of] how-much; ^{b}19 for it is from here that it has come
to the others [= the other genera]. ^{b}20 For measure is that
by which how-much is known; and how-much *qua* how-
much is known either by a unit or a number, and all number
[is known] by a unit, so that all how-much is known, *qua*
how-much, by the unit, and that by which how-muches are
primarily known, this itself is a unit. ^{b}23 Hence the unit is
the origin of number *qua* number. And from here in the
others [= in the other genera], too, 'measure' means that
primary thing by which each thing is known, and the
measure of each thing is a unit, in length, in breadth, in
depth, in weight, in speed. ('Weight' and 'speed' are common in both contraries*; for each of them is double [*ditton*],
as 'weight' is both that which has any amount of gravity
whatever and that which has an excess of gravity, and
'speed' is that which has any amount of movement whatever
and that which [has] an excess of movement; for there is
some speed even of the slow, and [some?] weight [even] of
the lighter).

^{52b}31 In all these, then, measure and principle [*arkhē*] is
something that is a unit and indivisible, since even in lines
they treat the one-foot-line as indivisible. ^{b}33 For everywhere they seek as measure something that is a unit and
indivisible; and this is the simple [*to haploun*] in either quality or quantity. Now, where it seems impossible to take away
or to add, this measure is exact (which is why ^{53a} [the mea-
sure] of number is most exact; for they posit the monad as
in every way indivisible); and in the others [= other cases]
they imitate this sort [of case]; for from a stade [= 200
yards] or a talent [= 6000 drachmas] or anything relatively

large, something added or taken away would more escape
notice than from something relatively small; **ᵃ5** so that the
primary thing from which, in respect of perception, this is
not possible, this everyone makes a measure, both of liquids
and of solids ["moists and drys"] and of weight and of size;
and they think they know the quantity when they know it
through this measure. **ᵃ8** And moreover, [they know] movement too by the simple movement and the quickest (for this
takes the least time); **ᵃ10** hence in astronomy a unit of this
sort is principle and measure (for they hypothesize to be uniform and fastest the movement of the heaven, with reference to which they calibrate the others), and in music the
quarter-tone [is the measure], because it's the smallest inter-
val, and in speech the phonetic element. **ᵃ13** And all these
are 'some unit' in this way: not in the sense of 'a unit' being
something common to them all, but in the way that has been
described.

53ᵃ14 But the measure is not always one in number, but
sometimes more than one, for example the quarter-tones are
two (not the tones as heard, but in the ratios), and the voiced
sounds by which we measure are several, and the diagonal
is measured by two measures*, and so are all spatial
magnitudes [measured by different 'units']. **ᵃ18** Thus, then,
"of all things is the 'unit' the measure", in that we get to
know the things 'out of which' the substance is, when we
divide either in respect of quantity or in respect of form.
ᵃ20 And the reason why the 'unit' is indivisible is just that
the primary [measure?] of each [of these] is indivisible.
ᵃ21 But not every [measure] is indivisible in the same way,
e.g. *foot* and *monad*; rather the latter is in every way [in-
divisible], the former has to be placed among the things that
are undivided in reference to perception, as has already
been said*, for probably everything that is continuous is
divisible.

53ᵃ24 The measure is always co-generic [*syn-genes*] [with
what is measured]; for [measure] of spatial magnitudes is a

spatial magnitude, and in particular [measure] of length is a length, of breadth a breadth, of voiced sound a voiced sound, of weight a weight, of monads a monad. ([a]27 For this last must be taken in this way, and *not* "of numbers a number"; this would indeed be necessary if the parallel held; but the claim is not really similar—it is as if it were claimed that the measure of monads is monads but not a monad; but number is a plurality of monads.)

53[a]31 Knowledge [*epistēmē*], also, we call a measure of things, and perception too, for the same reason: that we get to know something *by* them, since they really are measured more than they measure. But it strikes *us* as though someone else measured us and we got to know how big we are by the cubit-rule's applying to so-and-so-much of us.* [a]35 Protagoras says, "man is the measure of all things," as if 53[b] he'd said "the knowing [man]", or "the perceiving [man]"; these in that they have, one of them, perception, the other, knowledge, which we say are the measures of their objects [*hypokeimena*]. [b]3 Saying nothing, then, they [= who talk as Protagoras does] seem to be saying something exceptional.

53[b]4 It is evident, than, that the essence of unit, if defined according to [the meaning of] the name, is pre-eminently a certain measure, and above all of quantity, secondarily of quality; and one thing will be of this sort if it is indivisible in respect of quantity, another if in respect of quality; and hence that which is a unit is indivisible, either *simpliciter*, or *qua* unit.

Iota 2 ['One' and 'That which Is'. 'Unity' and 'Being'.]

53[b]9 With regard to the substance and the nature [of the one], we must investigate in which of two ways it stands, just as in the review of the aporematic problems* we approached What the 'one' Is and how* we must begin about it, whether we must take the one itself as being a certain substance (as

the Pythagoreans, earlier, and Plato, later, say), or whether
rather a certain nature underlies, and [the one] should be
given a more familiar [sort of] account and [an account]
more in the manner of those who write "On Nature"; for of
these one says the one is Love, another Air, another The
Apeiron.* **ᵇ16** If, then, none of the universals can be substance, as has been said in the writings on substance and on
being*, and if this [= being] itself cannot be substance in
the sense of some one thing alongside the many (for it is
common [to them all]), but is only a thing-predicated, plainly neither can the one [be substance]; for 'being' and 'one'
are predicated most universally of all. **ᵇ21** So that neither
are the genera certain natures or substances separate from
the other things, nor can 'the one' be a genus, for the same
reasons for which being and substance cannot [be genera].
ᵇ24 Further, the affair must stand similarly for all [cases?
things-predicated?]; but 'being' and 'one' are said in the
same number of ways; so that since among qualities the
'one' is something and some nature, and similarly too
among quantities, it's plain that it must be investigated in
general What the 'one' Is, just like What 'being' Is, as it is
not enough [to say] that its nature is just this ['one', or 'being']. **ᵇ28** Yet in fact among colors, the one is a color, e.g.
white, and then the others [= other colors] are seen to
come-to-be 'out of' this and black, and black is the lack
[*sterēsis*] of white, just as darkness is of light.

53ᵇ32 So that if the things that are were colors,
then the things that are would be a certain number,
but [a number] of what? Plainly, of colors, and the
unit would be a particular unit, e.g. white.

53ᵇ34 And similarly, if the things that are were
melodies, they would be a number, however this
time of quarter-tones, but the substance of them
would not be a number; and the unit would have
been something the substance of which was not
54ᵃ the unit but quarter-tone.

54ª1 And similarly, in the case of sounds, the things that are would be a number of phonetic elements, and the unit would be a vowel.

54ª3 And if [the things that are were] rectilinear figures, there would be a number of figures, and the unit would be the triangle.

ª4 And the same account applies to the other genera, so that since in the afflictions and in the qualities and in the quantities and in movement there are numbers and 'some unit', in all of them the number is 'a number of somethings' and the unit is 'one something', but the substance [of it?] is not this [= being one or a unit] itself, and it must stand similarly in the case of the substances, for it stands similarly in all cases.

54ª9 That the unit, then, is a certain [distinct] nature in every genus, and there is no thing whose nature is [just] this itself, the unit, is evident, but just as in colors the one-itself that must be investigated is one color, so also in substance the one-itself is one substance. **ª13** That 'one' and 'being' in a way mean the same, is plain, [i] by [their] corresponding to the categories in the same number of ways, and by [their] not being in any category (e.g. not in the what it is, not in the qualified, but it stands to them just as being does), and [ii] by the fact that nothing further is predicated in '[is] *one* man' than in '[is] (a) man' (just as 'being' is nothing further than what and qualified and quantified), and [iii] by the fact that *to be one* is *to be each thing* [or: the essence of one *is* the essence of each thing].

Iota 3 [One and many; same, like, equal; other, unlike, unequal.]

54ª20 The one [*to hen*] and the many [*ta polla*] are opposed [*antikeitai*] in several modes, one of which is that of
one : plurality° [*plēthos*] :: indivisible : divisible;
for that which is 'divided' or 'divisible' is said to be some

plurality [*plēthos ti*], but that which is 'indivisible' or 'not divided' [is called] one. ᵃ23 Then, since the oppositions [*antitheseis*] are fourfold, and of these [two terms, 'divisible' and 'indivisible'] one is said with respect to a lack [*kata sterēsin legetai*], they must be contraries [*enantia*], neither said as contradictory [*antiphasis*] nor as relatives [*hōs ta pros ti*]. ᵃ26 And the 'one' is called and revealed from the contrary, the indivisible from the divisible, because the plurality and the divisible is more perceptible than the indivisible, so that in formula the plurality is prior to the indivisible, by way of perception.

54ᵃ29 To the one, as we diagrammed it in the "Division of Contraries"*, belong the same, and like, and equal; to the plurality, the other, and unlike, and unequal.

54ᵃ32 "The *same*" being said in many ways, [1] one way we sometimes mean it is "[same] in respect of number"; [2] another way, if [the thing] is one both in formula and in number, e.g. you are one with yourself both in form and in matter; [3] again, if the formula 54ᵇ of the primary substance is one, e.g. equal straight lines are the same, and so are equal and equal-angled quadrilaterals; and indeed many more, but in these equality is oneness [*henotēs*].

54ᵇ3 Things are *like*, [1] if, while not being absolutely [*haplōs*] the same, nor without difference in respect of their composite substance, they are the same in respect of the form, as the larger square is 'like' the smaller, and unequal straight lines; for these are 'like', but they are not absolutely the same. ᵇ7 [2] Other things [are like] if, having the same form, and being things in which more and less occurs, they are neither more nor less. ᵇ9 [3] Other things [are like] if they are the same affliction and one in form, e.g. the white, to a greater and a lesser degree; they are said to be like because their form is one. ᵇ11 [4] Other things [are like] if they have more [afflictions] the same than different, either completely [*haplōs*] or the more obvious ones, e.g. tin [is 'like'] silver *qua* white*, and gold [is 'like'] fire *qua* yellow or flame-colored.

54ᵇ13 It is clear, therefore, that "other" and "unlike" also are said in many ways. [1] In one sense "other*" and "same" [are said] in opposite ways (which is why everything is either the same as or other than everything*); [2] in another sense [things are other] unless both the matter and the formula are one (which is why you are other than your neighbor); [3] in a third sense [things are other] as are the objects of mathematics*. **ᵇ17** "Other" and "same", then, can for this reason be said of everything with respect to everything—that is, the things of which 'one' and 'being' are said; for ["other"] is not contradictory of "same", which is why it is not applied to things that are not (to which "not the same" *is* applied), but it is applied to all the things that are; for such things as *are* and are *one* are by their nature either one or not one [with such things]*.

54ᵇ22 The other, then, and the same, are in this way opposed; but difference is not the same as otherness*. **ᵇ24** For the other, and that which it is other than, are not necessarily other *in something* [*heteron tini*]; for everything that is something that is, is either other or the same; but the different is different *from something, in something* [*tinos tini diaphoron*], so that it's necessary that there be something that is the same, *in which* they differ. **ᵇ27** And this, that is the same, is the genus or the species; for everything that differs, differs either in genus or in species, [1] in genus those things of which [a] the matter is not common, and [b] there is not coming-to-be into each other, e.g. things whose schema of predication is not the same*, [2] in species those things whose genus is the same (genus meaning that same thing which both of the different things are called in respect of substance).

54ᵇ31 The 'contraries' are 'different', and contrariety° is a sort of difference [*diaphora tis*]. That we are right to make this hypothesis is clear from induction; for all these [contraries] too are evidently different, not being merely other, but some are other in genus, whereas some again are in the same **55ª** column of predication, and therefore in the same

genus and the same in genus. [a2] It is distinguished elsewhere* what sorts of things are the same or other in genus.

Iota 4 [Contrariety, difference, possession, and lack.]

[55a3] Since things that 'differ' can differ from each other
more and less, there is also some greatest difference, and
this I call *contrariety*. That [contrariety] is the greatest difference, is clear from induction. [a6] For things that differ in
genus do not have a way to each other, but are too far dis-
tant, and not comparable; but for things that differ in
species, the comings-to-be are from the contraries as extremes, and the distance between the extremes is the
greatest, and therefore also that between the contraries.
[a10] But truly, that which is greatest in each genus is completion [*teleion*]. For that is greatest which cannot be exceeded,
and that is complete which nothing can be found outside of;
for the complete difference [*teleia diaphora*] has a completion [*telos*], just as the other things that are called complete
are so called by having [attained] a completion, and there is
nothing outside the completion; for in everything it is an extreme, and surrounds [the rest], which is why there is
nothing outside the completion, and that which is complete
is in need of nothing further.

[55a16] From these [considerations], then, it is clear that
contrariety is complete difference; but as the contraries are
said in many ways, the sense of "complete" will follow as
'being contraries' belongs to them.

[55a19] These things being so, it is plain that one thing cannot have more than one contrary (for neither can there be
anything more extreme than the extreme, nor can there be
more than two extremes of the one distance), and [it is
plain] in general that, if contrariety is difference, and if difference is between two things, therefore so is the complete
difference.

55ª23 The other definitions of contraries must also be true. For example, [1] the complete difference 'differs' the most (for no difference can be found 'further outside' the things that differ in genus and in species; for it has been shown* that with reference to the things outside the genus there is no 'difference', but this is the greatest difference between these [things in a given genus]), and [2] the things in the same genus that differ the most are contraries (for the complete difference is the greatest difference between these [things in a genus]), and **ª29** [3] the things in the same recipient [*dektikon*] that differ the most are contraries (for the matter is the same for [these] contraries), and [4] the things under [*hypo*] the same faculty [*dynamis*] that differ the most [are contraries] (for the science that deals with one genus is the same, and among the things [in the genus] the complete difference is the greatest [difference])*.

55ª33 The primary contrariety is that [between] *possession* [*hexis*] and *lack* [*sterēsis*]—not every lack (for "lack" is said in many ways), but that which is complete. The others will be called contraries with respect to these, some by 'possessing' [these], others by 'producing' or 'being productive of' [these], others by 'being acquisitions or losses of' these or of other contraries. **ª38** If, then, these things are opposed: contradiction, lack, **55ᵇ** contrariety, and relations, and of these the primary type is contradiction, and of contradiction there is no intermediate, while contraries do admit [intermediates], then it is clear that contradiction and contraries are not the same; **ᵇ3** but lack is a sort of contradiction; for either what is entirely incapable of 'possessing' [something], or what, being of a nature to possess it, still does not possess it, 'is lacking', either altogether, or in some determinate way (here already we are 'saying this in many ways', as we have distinguished elsewhere*), **ᵇ7** so that lack is a sort of contradiction or incapacity which is either determinate [*dioristheisa*] or associated [*syneilēmmenē*] with the recipient [*dektikon*]*; which is why there is

no intermediate for contradiction, but for some lack there
is; **ᵇ9** for on one hand everything is either equal or *not*
equal, but on the other hand not everything is either equal
or *un*equal, or if it is, it is only in that which is receptive of
the equal. **ᵇ11** If, then, the comings-to-be in the matter are
out of the contraries, and proceed either out of the form and
the possession [*hexeōs*] of the form, or out of some lack of
the form and the shape, it is clear that every lack must be a
contrariety, though presumably not every contrariety is a
lack* (the reason being that that which 'is lacking' may be
lacking in a variety of ways); for the *extremes* from which
the changes proceed, these are contraries.

55ᵇ17 And this is also evident through induction. For
every contrariety has a lack as one of its contraries*, but not
all in the same way; on one hand inequality [is contrary] of
equality, and unlikeness of likeness, but on the other hand
vice [is contrary] of virtue, and these differ in the way that
has been described*; **ᵇ21** it is one case if the thing simply is
lacking, it is another if [it has become lacking] at a certain
time or in a certain way (e.g. at a certain age or in the dominant part), or throughout; **ᵇ23** this is why in some cases
there is something between, and there is a man who is
neither good nor bad, and in others there is not, but
necessarily [a number] is either odd or even. **ᵇ25** Further,
some [contraries] have a determinate subject, and others do
not. Therefore it is evident that always one of the contraries
is said in respect of a lack; but it is enough if [this holds] for
the primary, i.e. the genera of opposites, e.g. the one and
the many; for the others reduce to these.

Iota 5 [Aporias: Equal, Large and Small.]

55ᵇ30 Since one thing has one contrary, one might raise
the aporia how the one is opposed to the many, and the equal
[opposed] to the large and the small. **ᵇ32** For if we say
"whether" [*poteron*] always [= only] in an antithesis, e.g.

"whether it is white or black" and "whether it is white or
not white" (we do not say "whether it is man or white",
unless we are proceeding on a hypothesis and inquiring, say,
"whether it was Cleon who came, or Socrates"—but this is
not [a] necessary [disjunction] in any genus; but even this
has come from that case [= of opposites]; for only opposites
cannot belong at the same time, which is used here, also, in
"which of them [poteros] came"; **56ª** for if it is possible [for
both to have come] at the same time, the question is
ludicrous; but if so, then even so it likewise falls into an antithesis, into 'the one or many', i.e. "whether both came or
one of the two"); **ª3** if, then, the inquiry of "whether" [tou
poterou] is always among opposites, and it is said [= asked]
"whether it is greater or less or equal", what is the opposi-
tion of the equal to these [= the other two]? **ª6** For it is not
contrary to either alone, nor to both; for [1] why [should it
be contrary] any more to the greater than to the less? Further, [2] the equal is contrary to the unequal, so that it will
be [contrary] to more than one thing. **ª8** But [3] if the unequal means the same as both [the greater and the less]
together, then [the equal] will be opposite to both (and the
aporia supports those who say that the unequal is a 'dyad'*),
but it follows that one thing is contrary to two; which is
impossible. **ª12** Further, it seems that the equal is intermediate between large and small, but no contrariety is seen to be
intermediate, nor by definition is it possible; for it would not
be complete if it were intermediate of anything*, but rather
it always has something intermediate within itself.

56ª15 It remains, then, that it is opposed either as a negation or as a lack. Now, it cannot be [a negation or lack] of
one of the two (for why of the large rather than the small?);
it is, therefore, the 'lacking' negation of both, which is also
why "whether" is said with reference to both, and not with
reference to one of the two (e.g., "whether greater or
equal", "whether equal or less"), but there are always three
[cases]. **ª20** But it is not a lack from necessity; for not

everything is 'equal' that is not greater or less, but only those things to which these naturally pertain.

56ª22 The equal, then, is that which is neither large nor small, but is of a nature to be large or small; and it is opposed to both as a 'lacking' negation, and therefore is intermediate [between them]. And that which is neither good nor bad is opposed to both, but is nameless; for each of these is said in many ways and the recipient [of them] is not one; rather 'that which is neither white nor black' would be more [one]. **ª27** But neither is this called 'one', however the things [= the colors] in the case of which this negation is 'lackingly' said [i.e., where the negation causes the lack] are in a way limited; for they must be either gray or ochre or something else like that. **ª30** Therefore those people criticize incorrectly, who think that all things are said alike, so that between shoe and hand, there will be an intermediate, 'that which is neither shoe nor hand', on the ground that 'that which is neither good nor bad' [is intermediate between] the good and the bad—as if there will be something intermediate in all cases. **ª34** But this does not necessarily follow. For one case is the joint denial of opposites between which there is a certain intermediate and there naturally pertains a certain distance; **56ᵇ** but between the other two there is no 'difference'*' for the things whose denials are joined are in different genera, so that the subject is not one.

Iota 6 [Aporias: One and Many.]

56ᵇ3 One might also get into aporias in a similar way about the one and the many. For if the many are opposed to the one *simpliciter*, several impossibilities follow. For [1] the one will be little or few, for the many are opposed also to the few. Further, [2] the two will be many, since the double is multiple but is said in respect of two; therefore the one [will be] few; for in relation to what are two many, except in relation to one and [hence] few? For there is nothing less

[= 'fewer']. ᵇ10 Further, [3] if what holds in length with
long and short, holds also in plurality with many and few,
and if whatever is 'much' (*polu*) is also 'many' (*polla*), and
the 'many' are 'much' (unless, indeed, there is a difference
in the case of something continuous and easily-bounded),
then the few will be some plurality. ᵇ13 Therefore the one is
some plurality, i.e. if it is also few; but it must be this [=
few], if the two are many. But it may be that the 'many' are
in a sense also said to be 'much', but with a difference: as,
'water is *much*, but not *many*'. ᵇ16 But 'many' is applied to
such things as are divisible, in one sense if there is a plurality
that has an excess, either *simpliciter* or relatively (and
similarly 'few' is a plurality having a deficiency), but in
another sense as number, and it is in this sense alone that it
is opposed to the one. ᵇ20 Thus we say 'one or many', just
as if one said 'one and ones', or 'white thing and white
things', or referred the things measured* to the measure; in
this way multiples are so called also; for each number is
'many' because of ones and because each number is
measurable by one, and [it is 'many'] in the sense of that
which is opposed to the one, not to the little or few. ᵇ25 In
this sense, then, even the two is many, but in the sense of 'a
plurality that has an excess, either relatively or *simpliciter*'
it is not, but it is the first [plurality]. ᵇ27 But taken *simpliciter*, the two are few; for it is the first plurality having a
deficiency (hence Anaxagoras left the topic incorrectly, saying that

> All things were together, boundless (*apeira*) both
> in plurality and in smallness. . . .

where he ought to have said, instead of "in smallness", "in
fewness"; for they [could] not [be] boundless [in few-
ness]*), since the few is not due to the one, as some say, but
due to the two.

56ᵇ32 Among numbers, then, the one is opposed to the
many as measure to measurable; and these [are opposed] in
the manner of relatives, which are not relatives in respect of

themselves. We have distinguished elsewhere* that relatives are said in two ways, some [1] as contraries, others [2] as knowledge is referred to the knowable, where something is called [relative] because ^{57a} another is referred to it. Nothing prevents the one from being less than something, such as two; for it is not the case that if it is less, it is also few. ^{a2} Plurality is as it were the genus of number; for number is plurality measurable by one, and the one and number are in a sense opposed, not as contrary, but as certain relatives have been said [to be opposed]; for insofar as one is measure and the other measurable, in that way they are opposed, which is why not everything that is one is a number, e.g. if a thing is indivisible [it is not a number]. ^{a7} But while knowledge is said to be similarly relative to the knowable, it does not turn out similarly. For while knowledge may seem to be the measure and the knowable what is measured, it happens to be the case that all knowledge is something knowable but not everything that is knowable is knowledge, because in a certain way knowledge is measured by the knowable. ^{a12} Plurality is contrary neither to the little—rather to this the much [is contrary], as plurality that exceeds to plurality that is exceeded—nor in all ways to the one; but in one way [it is contrary to the one], as has been said, in that it is divisible and the other [= the one] indivisible, but in another way they are relative, as knowledge is to the knowable, if [plurality] is number and the one is a measure.

Iota 7 [Contraries and intermediates within a genus.]

^{57a18} Since there can be an intermediate of contraries and of some there is [such], it is necessary that the intermediates be [composed] 'out of' the contraries. For all intermediates are in the same genus as that which they are intermediates

of. **ᵃ21** For we call those things intermediates into which
that which changes must change sooner [*proteron*] (e.g., if
one proceed from the highest [string] to the lowest by
smallest intervals one will come sooner to the intermediate
tones; and in colors, [proceeding] from white to black one
will come sooner to purple or gray than to black; and likewise for the other cases). **ᵃ26** But to change from one genus
into another genus is not possible except per accidens, as
'from a color to a shape'. Necessarily, therefore, intermediates must be in the same genus both as each other and as that
which they are intermediates of.

57ᵃ30 But all intermediates are between opposites of some
sort; for 'out of' these alone can changes take place 'in
respect of themselves' (hence an intermediate is impossible
between things that are not opposites, for then there would
be a change that was not 'out of' opposites). **ᵃ33** Of opposites, there is no intermediate of contradiction (for this is
what contradiction is, an antithesis of which one side or the
other must be present [in anything], not having any intermediate), of the others, some are relative, some are lack,
and some are contrary. **ᵃ37** Of relatives, those that are not
contraries do not have intermediates; the reason is that they
are not in the same genus. For what **57ᵇ** could be intermediate between knowledge and knowable? But between large
and small [there is an intermediate].

57ᵇ2 If intermediates are in the same genus, as has been
shown, and are intermediates of contraries, then necessarily
they are composed 'out of' these contraries. For either there
will be some genus of them or none. And if there is to be a
genus in such a way as to be something prior [*proteron*] to
the contraries, then the differentiae that constituted
["made"] the contrary species-as-of-a-genus will be contraries prior [to these species]; for the species are 'out of'
the genus and the differentiae (**ᵇ8** e.g., if white and black
are contraries, and one is 'diacritic color' and the other is

'syncritic color'*, then these differentiae— 'diacritic' and 'syncritic'—are prior; so that these are contraries to one another that are prior). **ᵇ11** But, the [species?] that are differentiated contrarily are more contrary; and the other [species], i.e. the intermediates, will be 'out of' the genus and the differentiae (e.g., all colors that are intermediate between white and black must be said to be 'out of' the genus—the genus is 'color'—and 'out of' certain differentiae; **ᵇ16** but these will not be the primary contraries; otherwise, every color will be either white or black; therefore they are other [than the primary contraries]; therefore they will be intermediate between the primary contraries; and the primary differentiae are the 'diacritic' and the 'syncritic'); **ᵇ19** so that it is about these contraries that are not within a genus* that it must first be asked, 'out of what' their intermediates are [composed] (for necessarily things that are in the same genus either are 'out of' things of which the genus is not a component, or else are incomposite). Now, contraries are not composed 'out of' one another, therefore they are origins; but the intermediates are either all [incomposite], or none. **ᵇ23** But 'out of' the contraries something comes-to-be, so that there will be change into this before [there is change] into them; for there will be less of the one and more of the other. **ᵇ26** This too, therefore, will be intermediate between the contraries. All the other intermediates, therefore, are compounds too; for that which is 'more of this, less of that' is a compound in some way 'out of' those things 'this and that' which it is said to be 'more and less of'. **ᵇ29** And since there are no other things of the same genus [*homogenē*] that are prior to the contraries, all the intermediates must be 'out of' the contraries, so that all the things beneath [*ta katō panta*], both the contraries and the intermediates, will be 'out of' the primary contraries. **ᵇ32** It is clear, then, that intermediates are all in the same genus, and intermediate between contraries, and all composed 'out of' the contraries.

Iota 8   [Differentia: Otherness in species as otherness of genus.]

57ᵇ35 That which is 'other in species' is other *than something*, [and] *another something**, and the latter must belong to both, as, if an animal is other in species [than another], both are animals. Necessarily, therefore, the things that are other in species are in the same genus; for here is what I call genus: that thing by which both are called one and the same thing, and **58ᵃ** which is differentiated, not per accidens, whether as matter or otherwise. For not only must the common [character] belong, as both are animals, but this animal itself must also be other for each, as, one is horse, the other is man, which is why this common [character] must be other than the others in species.* **ᵃ5** They will be, then, in respect of themselves, one, an animal of *this* sort, the other, [an animal] of *this* sort, for example, one, *horse*, the other, *man*. Necessarily, therefore, this differentia is an otherness of the genus. For by 'differentia of the genus' I mean an otherness that makes the genus itself other.

ᵃ8 This [differentia], then, will be a contrariety, as is also clear by induction; for all things are divided by opposites, and it has been shown* that contraries are in the same genus; for contrariety was a complete differentia, and all difference in species is difference *of something*, [and] *a different something*, so that the latter is the same for both and is genus (which is why also all contraries which are different in species and not in genus are in the same column of predication*, and other than one another to the maximum—for the difference is complete—and cannot come to be together with one another). The differentia, therefore, is a contrariety.

ᵃ17 This, therefore, is what it is for things to be 'other in species'—it is, their being the same in genus, having contrariety, being indivisible (*atoma*) (and those things are the same in species that do not have contrariety, being indivis-

ible); for in division, contrarieties arise even in the intermediate stages before getting to the indivisibles; so that it is
apparent that with reference to what is called the genus,
none of the species-as-of-a-genus [cf. Iota 7 57^{b}7] is either
the same as it, or other than it in species (appropriately; for
the matter is revealed by negation, and the genus is the matter of that of which it is called the genus—not as that [=
genus = family] of the Heraclidae, but as that [= genus] in
the nature of a thing), nor is it thus with reference to the
things not in the same genus, but it will differ from them in
genus, and [differ] in species from things in the same genus.
^{a}26 For necessarily, the difference of a thing from that from
which it differs in species, must be a contrariety; and this
belongs only to the things that are in the same genus.

Iota 9 [Aporia: What contrarieties make otherness in species?]

^{58a}29 One might raise the aporia why woman does not differ from man in species, female and male being contrary
and the difference a contrariety*, [and why] neither are a
female and a male animal other in species, even though this
difference [belongs] to animal in respect of itself, and not as
pallor or darkness does, but female and male belong *qua*
animal. ^{a}34 This aporia is almost the same as [the one that
goes]: why does one contrariety make things other in
species, but another not, as footed and winged do, but pallor
and darkness do not? Is it that the former are afflictions proper [*oikeia*] to the genus, but the latter less so? And since
^{58b} one [element] is formula and one is matter, contrarieties
that are in the formula make a difference in species, but
those that are in the thing composited with the matter do not
make one. ^{b}3 Hence pallor of a man does not make [a difference of species], or darkness, nor is there a differentia
with respect to species between the pale man and the dark
man, not even if a single word is assigned [to each].* ^{b}5 For

the man [is here taken] as material, and matter does not make a differentia; for this reason the [individual] men are not species of man, even though the fleshes and the bones 'out of which' this and this man are, are other; but the composite is other, but not other in species, because in the formula there is no contrariety. **b9** This [= species] is the ultimate indivisible; Callias is the formula with the matter; so also is the pale man, then, because Callias is pale; and so man [is pale], per accidens. **b12** Nor, then, do a brazen circle and a wooden one [differ in species]; nor do a brazen triangle and a wooden circle differ in species because of the matter, but because there is a contrariety present in the formula. **b15** But does the matter not make things other in species, when it is other in some way, or is there a way in which it does? For why is *this* horse other in species than *this* man, although the formulae of them includes the matter? Or is it because a contrariety is present in the formula? For [there is a contrariety] also between a pale man and a dark horse, and in species at that, but not *qua* the one is pale and the other is dark, since even if both had been pale, they would have been other in species in any case. **b21** Male and female are afflictions proper [*oikeia*] to animal, but not in respect of the substance, but in the matter, i.e. the body, which is why the same seed becomes female or male when afflicted in a certain way. It has been stated, then, what it is to be other in species, and why some things differ in species, and others do not.

Iota 10 [Perishable and imperishable must be other in kind.]

58b25 Since contraries are other in form, and the perishable and the imperishable are contraries (for a lack is a determinate incapacity), the perishable and the imperishable must necessarily be other in kind*. **b29** Now then, we have been speaking of universal names themselves, so that

it might appear not to be necessary that everything imperishable and [everything] perishable be other in form, just as
not [every] pale thing [is other in form than every] dark
thing (for the same thing can be both, and at the same time
if it is universal, as man can be both pale and dark, and as
for individuals,* the same man can also, not at the same
time, be pale and dark, even though the pale is contrary to
the dark); but while, of contraries, some belong to some
things per accidens, such as [both] those just mentioned and
many others, other [contraries] [59a] cannot, among which
are the perishable and the imperishable; for nothing is
perishable per accidens; for what is per accidens is capable
of not belonging, but the perishable is among the things that
belong of necessity to what they belong to; or else one and
the same thing will be perishable and imperishable, if the
perishable were capable of not belonging to it. [a6] The
perishable must therefore either be the substance or belong
to the substance of each perishable thing. And the same account holds also for the imperishable; for both are things
that hold of necessity. [a9] Therefore, to the extent that and
in respect of which primarily one thing is perishable and
another thing imperishable, they contain an antithesis, so
that they must necessarily be other in kind. It is evident,
then, that there cannot be forms of the sort that some people
say; for then one man will be perishable and another imperishable. [a13] Even so, the forms are said to be the same in
form with the particulars [*tois tisi*], and not homonyms; but
things that are other in kind are farther apart than those that
are other in form.

Notes

Zeta 1

28ª10. (1) A chronic difficulty in the rendering of *to on* is its ambivalence as between:

that which is (as in the plural, *ta onta*, the being*s* or the things that are—either the existents, or 'the things that are' e.g. good, bad, man, god, healthy), and

being (as in the be-ing *of* the beings—either their existence, or their being e.g. good, bad, man, god, healthy).

A parallel ambivalence holds for *ousia*, as between:

that which is a substance (e.g., some man, some god), and

the 'substance *of*' such a thing.

The identification and analysis of substance in this latter sense is a major objective of Book Zeta.

(2) As a rule in this work, both that which 'is said' (*legetai*) or is something 'said' (*legomenon*) and that which 'is predicated' (*katēgoreitai*) or is a 'thing-predicated' (*katēgoroumenon* 28ª13, *katēgorēma* 28ª33) are some sort of *on*, thing that is, rather than a linguistic expression, a "predicate" in the linguistic sense, or the like. (There seems to be no significant difference between *katēgoroumenon* and *katēgorēma*.)

28ª20. An *a-poria* is a difficulty, taking the form of one's not being able to find a "way through", or *poros* (whence "pore"). The verb, *aporeō*, is "I am at a loss", "I can't find my way". (*Eu-poria* is "clear sailing", "easy passage".) The phrase *tis aporēseien* is thus to be understood, "someone might get into difficulties with" or "be puzzled over". In the *Metaphysics* it hardly ever is used in the dialectical vein of the *Topics*, in the sense of posing a problem to confound one's debating opponent, still less a trick or trap question. Occasionally it is used mockingly, as for the philosophical I-don't-understand as practiced by "the Antistheneans and like ignoramuses", Eta 3 43^{b}23 ff.

28^{a}36-^{b}2. "We think we *eidenai* each thing when we *gnōnai* what it is", twice.

Zeta 2
28^{b}8-13. There is a strong implicit reference to this first suggestion as to "what things are substances" in Zeta 16, first sentence; see note on 40^{b}9.

Zeta 3
28^{b}35-36. *Hypo-keimenon* (first occurrence at Zeta 1 28^{b}26) is the word translated "subject" in the *Categories*; it has to be understood as trading on its literal compound meaning as 'something *under-lying*'. In the *Categories*, the identification of the substances as the most basic *subjects* of all things-predicated is highly explicit and emphatic: *Cats.* 2^{b}15-17, 2^{b}37-3^{a}1.

28^{b}36-29^{a}2. This is a fairly close paraphrase of *Cats.* 2^{b}37-3^{a}1.

29^{a}5. There is little difference in practice between *synolon* and *syntheton*; I have adopted "composite" and "compound", respectively, as conventional renderings.

29^{a}11-12. The idea of the thought-experiment is that if everything is 'stripped off' that has the form of a *katēgorou-menon*, i.e. of something predicated of anything, then what is 'left over' will be the 'ultimate subject', in the sense stipulated above at 28^{b}36-37.

29^{b}3-13. The apparent sense has been rendered, "more known to oneself", i.e. familiar, versus "more knowable by nature", i.e. intelligible. The alternative would be to render *gnōrimōteron* everywhere as "more knowable".

Zeta 4

29^{b}2. "The essence" traditionally translates *to ti ēn einai*, "the what it is to be" for a thing; the Greek is a technical coinage, very likely going back to the Academy (judging from its prominence in the *Topics*), that is employed to designate *just what is articulated by a definition* of a thing. (Cf., e.g., Zeta 4 30^{a}7, Zeta 5 31^{a}12, Eta 1 42^{a}17.) Thus as the notion of the content of a *definition* evolves from the *Topics* onward, the notion of 'essence' develops correspondingly.

29^{b}13. The ten-line jump from ^{b}3 to ^{b}13 is due to the relocation of the intervening lines of the Bekker text to the end of Zeta 3, proposed by Bonitz and followed by most editors since; see Ross *AM* ii 166. For a different reconstruction, due to von Arnim, see Owens, *DOB*[2] 347 & n.

29^{b}14-15. Locutions of the form "being F_d" ("being you$_d$", "being pale$_d$") translate Aristotle's corresponding idiom with the term *F* in the dative case: its probable ancestor is the expression "the what it is to be for F_d" (cf. note on 29^{b}2 above), in which F is also dative. Your being musical is just your having music-in-you, 'by way of coinciding'; but if being you$_d$ is being musical$_d$, then music must be part or all of the essence of you. That in turn entails that if you are a substance, then musical must be part or all of the substance *of* you, or else being musical$_d$ is what the *music* is, and if you are that$_d$, then presumably you are a quality.

(It should be noted in passing that 'musical' in ancient Greek does not center on melody and harmony. It means being versed in the legacy of the Muses, i.e. in the traditional codification of the culture, especially as embodied in the classical poets. Thus it is sometimes, and appropriately, Englished as 'educated' or 'cultured'.)

29^{b}15. According to *APo* i 4 73^{a}37 ff., an item X can belong to a subject S *kath' hauto* or 'in respect of itself' (that is, in respect of S), in the following two ways among others: either (1) X is in the *ti esti* of S (as X = twofooted or animal,

S = man), or (2) X is such that S is in the *ti esti* of X (as X = male/female or man, S = animal). (These are not the only senses of *kath' hauto*, but they are the two senses that make a *contrast* with *kata symbebēkos*.) It seems that sense (1) is intended here, since the effect of $29^b16\text{-}19$ is evidently to exclude sense (2). (For pale having surface in its *ti esti* see e.g. Delta 18 $1022^a16\text{-}17$, also—at least by implication— Eta 6 $45^b15\text{-}16$.)

From $29^b14\text{-}15$ and 17-18, it appears that if E = your essence, then *being you*$_d$ = *being E*$_d$.

29^b19.   The Greek says only, "because it's added on" (*hoti pros-estin auto*), leaving it ambiguous what the offending thing-added-on is. The reasoning of $29^b16\text{-}19$ may be: The second sense of 'in respect of itself' (note on 29^b15), illustrated by X = pale and S = surface, where S is in the definition of X, cannot be the applicable sense here, we are told, because *being a surface* isn't, as required for this sense, the *same* as *being pale* (only a kind of necessary condition of it). (In fact, a more basic criticism would be: being a surface isn't even a *way* of being pale, rather the other way round. See on *hoper* in note on $30^a2\text{-}7$ below.) In that case, the thought then arises, perhaps *being a pale*$_d$ *surface*$_d$ might belong to pallor 'in respect of itself' (in some sense that could advance the discussion), and represent exactly *what it is to be pale*$_d$? The answer to this is: No, the statement of the essence of something S must not contain the name S; the addition of "pale$_d$" spoils the attempted definition of "pale", by putting the definiendum in the would-be definiens. (This interpretation fits well with the lines that follow, but diverges from that of Ross (*AM* ii 168), who thinks "being a pale$_d$ surface$_d$" at $^b18\text{-}19$ is another attempt—which, if so, would have to be an awfully foolish one—at defining "*surface*".) Cf. also the next note.

29^b20.   As usual when *definition* comes up in Aristotle, the discussion is awash in use/mention difficulties; but the principles laid down in the immediately preceding lines and here being epitomized are too important to leave in their present condition. Thus let us for the moment distinguish between a substance, X, and the name of the substance, "X". Anticipating forthcoming developments, let us think of definition in terms of species being analyzed by way of genus and differentiae, GD (cf. below, 30^a11). Then one way of understanding a definition of the substance X, will be as an equation in which the name of X appears as what is nowadays called definiendum, and an expression naming the genus as differentiated appears as definiens: an equation of the form, "X = GD". If the definition is correct, (1) what is named by the expressions on the two sides of " = " must be *identical*, and (2) the definiens (called "the logos of the essence", 29^b20) must *explicate* ("formulate") the essential nature that is only *named* by the definiendum—and in particular, as a consequence, the definiens may not contain an occurrence of the definiendum itself (these two requirements, in reverse order, are the gist of 29^b19-20). It is very important to the line of argument being undertaken at this point in Zeta that in a *definition* "X = GD" of the essence of something, *one* thing is under study (not two); the identity is *strictly* understood; *zōion dipoun* is *what* Man is, it's not a second thing. Cf. further note on Zeta 6 32^a11.

29^b23. *syntheta* ("compounds") vs. *synola* ("composites"): see note on Zeta 3, 29^a5.

29^b29-30^a2 is difficult; here is one suggestion. A contrast is about to be drawn below (cf. 30^a4, 11, also Zeta 6 31^b13) between X said of Y *per se* ("in respect of itself", *kath' hauto*) and *per aliud* ("of something else", *allo kat' allou*). Now, a pale$_a$ man clearly is going to be sorted in the second class, as one thing (some pallor$_n$ or other) attaching to another thing (some man or other). On that basis, the passage points out, there are actually two ways in which a pale$_a$ man's being "not *kath' hauto*" (and thus, the doctrine will go, not properly definable) may be blundered into by someone trying to make definitions. (i) He is trying to define pale$_d$ (= pallor$_n$), a legitimate endeavor, but defines it as pale$_a$ man, which is an "attachment". Or (ii) he is trying to define pale$_a$ man ("cloak"), misguidedly, but also defines it as pale$_a$, producing a true *predication*, but no definition ("a pale man is indeed pale", but is not the essence for anything). (It can be seen that I have been unsuccessful in finding a way to read 29^{b}22-30^{a}2 without the definer's turning out to look quite silly.)

30^{a}2-7.   In the *Organon*, "X is *hoper* Y" is regularly used as a variant for "X is a species of the genus Y", and by no means exclusively in the category of substance (e.g., Justice is *hoper* Good, *Top*. iii 6 116^{a}23-28; Knowledge is *hoper* Opinion, iv 6 128^{a}33-37; etc.). Thus for species S and genus G, "S is *hoper* G" has to be translated, not too transparently, as "S is just what is (a) G", and "S is *hoper* G *ti*" as "S is just what is some G" —or a particular G"; the idea it expresses is, "S is one *form* of G", "S is one of the things being G comes to", "being S is a *way* of being G". (For some reason *X is hoper Y* is persistently mis-rendered "X is just what *Y* is", which gets the idea backwards; for the right rendering cf. Barnes, *APo* 83^{a}1 n. (p. 168), following Bonitz, *Index* 533^{b}19-534^{a}23 s.v. *hosper*.)

30^{a}7-10.   I.e., take that 24-book-long formula (*logos*), starting *mēnin aeide thea* "Sing the wrath, goddess", and ending *taphon Hektoros hippodamoio* "burial of Hector, breaker of horses", that corresponds to the name, "*The Iliad*". On the stated criterion, that formula or logos would count as a definition of the name, which is regarded as showing without further argument that the understanding of "meaning the same" involved in the criterion is unacceptably weak.

30^{a}12.   "Species of a genus", i.e., *haper tode*, cf. note on 30^{a}2-7.

30^{a}19.   Note in *sēmainei tēn ousian kai tode ti* ("means the substance and the 'some this' "), how the expression *tode ti*, commonly a stand-in for *ho tis anthrōpos* ("the individual man"), here is doubling between *anthrōpos tis* (individual) and *zōion ti* (species).

30ª32-34. An interpolated expansion of ª32-34: "For necessarily either these [i.e. substances, qualities, quantities, and their respective essences] are called 'beings' homonymously, or else by adding and taking away [i.e. adding and taking away qualifications on "being"—as that substances are beings *simpliciter*, nonsubstances in qualified senses], just as [they say] 'the unknown is known' [in a qualified sense, i.e. being known *to be unknown*]. . . ."

30ª34-b3. *pros hen*. Things that are called by the same name but in different meanings are sometimes said by Aristotle to be *homonyms*; an example, using names of modern English, would be the banks, which comprise the river banks and the savings banks. In the *Categories*, things called by the same name in the *same* meaning are said to be *synonyms*; in the present paragraph of Zeta 4, this is styled "being said *in respect of* one thing" (*kath' hen*); an example would be the men (= *anthrōpoi*, human beings). A third case, here styled "being said *with reference to* one thing" (*pros hen*), is that in which things are called by the same name in meanings that are different, yet also systematically related to a central and primary meaning; the commonest everyday example is the things that are healthy (for the standard exposition, see Gamma 2). The idea that *being* or *that which is* is itself a *pros hen legomenon* has already been introduced in the first two sentences of Zeta 1, but *pros to auto kai hen* here at 30ª35-b1 is the first use in Zeta of the actual technical term.

30b3-4. The "two ways" are (1) in terms of "adding and taking away qualifications" on 'being' in the categories of substance and non-substance, and (2) in terms of 'being' being said 'with reference to' a single thing (*pros hen*).

30b4-7. Note that in the discussion from 30ª17 to this point, a change of doctrine relative to the *Cats.* theory has been decided upon. In the *Cats.*, definition (and by implication, essence, cf. note on 29^{b}2, though the term itself is there little used) applies equally to substance and nonsubstance: White (= Whiteness), no less than Man, has a definition of What It Is, and the chief difference has to do with whether the definition (better perhaps: "definiens", cf. note on 29^{b}20) is or is not predicable of that which what it defines is predicated of (to which the answer is that the definition is predicable of that which what it defines is said-of (2^{a}19-21), but not of that which what it defines inheres in (2^{a}30-34, 3^{a}16-17)). We are here being told that in a "primary and unqualified" sense, only substances have definitions and essences, and nonsubstances only in a derivative and qualified way. This idea receives further elaboration as the discussion proceeds.

Zeta 5

30^{b}20.   As far as I can see, it is simply a mistake to say that there is any sense in which concavity belongs to nose in respect of itself, since neither is in the *ti esti* of the other (Zeta 4, note on 29^{b}15), and the relationship of concavity to a nose also is not that of a *kath' hauto symbebēkos* as defined e.g. at *APo* i 4 73^{b}10-16. See note on 31^{a}14. Perhaps "the concavity" means "*this* concavity" and is intended to be understood just *as* snubness.

30^{b}23.   I.e. the "other sense" of "in respect of itself", Zeta 4 above, 29^{b}19 and note on 29^{b}15.

31^{a}3.   There are textual difficulties in this line; I follow Bonitz (see OCT a.c., p. 136).

31^{a}14.   *Background note.* These "aporias" relate to terms that are "coupled" in the sense that they either (a) in general, are predicates carrying restrictions as to the subjects they can modify, or (b) in particular, indicate a *form* that carries or implies restrictions on the kind of *matter* that can 'take' that form. Favorite example: *concavity* can characterize surfaces of all sorts, maybe even immaterial (geometers') ones (cf. *Meta*. Epsilon 1 1025^b28 ff.); but *snubness* has to be concavity in a nose. (This is the "other sense" of "in respect of itself" in Zeta 4, because for snubness, as opposed to concavity, nose is in the *ti esti*.) Then the question is: is there an essence for such things? The importance of this is not local to "snub" but is global: (*Meta*. Epsilon 1 *ibid*.) "*all* the natural things are said (or 'are called what they are') like the snub, e.g. nose eye face flesh bone, and generally *animal*, and leaf root bark, and generally *plant*—for the formulae of none of these things are independent of movement but always include a matter." Cf. also Zeta 11 36^b21-32, and notes to 36^b25, 36^b30. Note that the "problem" of 30^b28 ff. partly turns on not distinguishing snub_a from snub_n or snubness, as is done for white_a, white_n in Zeta 6 below (31^b22-28).

Zeta 6

31^a19-24. Perhaps the argument intended is this: to show that (a) pale man is distinct from the essence of pale man, suppose the opposite, so that

(1) pale man = essence of pale man.

But (2)   (a) man = (a) pale man (if he's pale, that is) [Implicitly:

Therefore, (3)   man = essence of pale man (from the above).

But (4)   man = essence of man (obtained by dropping "pale" from (1), or better, at least on one interpretation, obtained from (II) below—i.e., from metaphysical first principles).

Therefore,]

(5) essence of man = essence of pale man.

But (5) is absurd, so supposition (1) is impossible. Aristotle at once proceeds to criticize this argument on the ground that at most a per accidens unity is furnished by (2), so that thenceforward only a very weak identity survives and the alleged *reductio ad adsurdum* is compromised. Probably he thinks that (5) is absurd even on the "weak" construal of " = " (Nicholas White has suggested this to me).

31ª24-28. This time something like the following may be contemplated:

           (1)   pale man = essence of pale man
(as before)

           (2)   (a) man = (a) pale man (as before).
   Therefore (3)   man = essence of pale man
(as before).

Furthermore (1′) musical man = essence of musical man
           (2′)   (a) man = (a) musical man
   Therefore (3′)   man = essence of musical man.
   Therefore (4)
       essence of pale man = essence of musical man
               (3, 3′).

   Therefore, (5)
       essence of pale = essence of musical (4).

This alleged *reductio* is, of course, even weaker than the first, as Aristotle seems to concede.

31ª28. It can be seen from both of these arguments about the non-identity of things "said per accidens" with their (supposed) essences, which indeed hardly make sense on any other construal (see premise (2) in both), that what is shown is the non-identity of the (supposed) 'essence of pale man' with *a pale man*. But what would be parallel with the approach about to be taken towards the identity of things "said per se" or in respect of themselves with their (approved) essences, would be fix upon the (supposed) *kind* or *species* pale man, and ask after the identity or non-identity of *it* (not some individual pale man) with its (supposed) essence. It is after all part of the teaching of Zeta 6 that even the individual man is not identical with the (approved) essence of man—at least I take it so, see note on 32ª11.

31ᵇ2. Here following the OCT "more substance"; on Ross's text, "and those substances will be prior".

31^{b}6-7. "It is *epistēmē* of each thing when we *gnōnai* the essence of that thing."

31^{b}14. *N.B.*! For the contrast of these alternatives, "of itself" *versus* "of another", cf. Z 4 30^{a}4, 11; for a reformulation of the question in different terms that is claimed to advance the analysis significantly, cf. Zeta 17 41^{a}25-^{b}11 and note on 41^{a}25-26.

31^{b}21. *Ekthesis*, cf. Ross, *AM* ii 178-9 and his note on A 9 992^{b}10 (*AM* i 208-9).

31^{b}22-28. The "double signification" is the use of "pale" to refer to the pale thing, and to refer to the color. Cf. *Categories* 5 2^{a}27-34, 3^{a}15-17.

32^{a}11. The doctrine of this chapter is more straightforward and plausible than are some of the arguments, and many of the interpretive problems arise from an ambiguity as to the relation intended by the expression "essence *of* X", and its converse, "X *having* an essence".

Standardly, "essence" is simply that which is articulated by a *definition* of anything (e.g. *Top.* i 4 101^{b}21, i 5 101^{b}38, i 8 103^{b}10, vi 1 139^{a}33, vii 3 153^{a}15, vii 5 154^{a}31, and just now Zeta 4, see 30^{a}3-7 (and notes on 29^{b}2, 29^{b}20, Zeta 5 31^{a}7-11, Eta 1 42^{a}17). Also standardly, there is no definition of individuals (this goes back to Plato, and cf. e.g. Zeta 10 36^{a}2-8, Zeta 15 39^{b}27-40^{a}7).

It follows that there are no essences *of* individuals, i.e., individuals do not *have* essences. And this is correct, on the appropriate understanding of "of" and "have": there is no definition of Socrates, and hence no essence "of" Socrates that he "has" all to himself; on the other hand he certainly may be thought to "have" those essential properties that he cannot cease to "have" without perishing, and so on another construal he may be said to "have" an essence after all. Zeta 6 shows that the problem here is not merely terminological.

There are three titles to deal with here: (1) Man, which is what gets the definition, (2) the essence of Man, which is what the definition articulates, and (3) Socrates the

individual man, who is not definable but who must *satisfy*
the definition that (1) gets, whatever that may be (on pain of
perishing, indeed).

Aristotle uses the expression "essence of X" (i.e., of
course, the Greek for this) *both for a relation between (2)
and (1), and for a relation between (2) and (3).* It is clear that
these are not the same relation. For (1) and (2) stand in the
relation of identity, in particular in the relation of *a specific
kind* to *itself as definitionally analyzed.* Whereas, the relationship of (2) to (3) certainly is not identity; its *Categories*
antecedent is the "predicability of the (specific) definition"
of the substantial individual, and its *Metaphysics* working-
out is highly complex. For now, it is enough to see the difference between the sense of "having" and "of" in which
the kind Man "has"$_{(1-2)}$ an essence, which is the essence
"of"$_{(2-1)}$ Man, and the sense in which Socrates "has"$_{(3-2)}$
an essence, which is the essence "of"$_{(2-3)}$ Socrates. It is the
plausible doctrine of Zeta 6 that the relation "essence
of"$_{(2-1)}$ between essence and kind *is* the relation of identity,
and that the relation "essence of"$_{(2-3)}$ between essence and
composite individual *is not.* (The second conjunct is not
stated explicitly, but I infer it to be the line intended on the
question "whether Socrates and essence of Socrates are the
same" (32^a8). Namely, No, Of Course Not. For the essence
"of"$_{(2-3)}$ Socrates is, of course, the essence "of"$_{(2-1)}$ Man.
That essence certainly is determinative of Socrates in highly
important ways, but it and Socrates cannot possibly be the
same thing.)

The very problem of Zeta 6, "What things are identical
with *their* essences?", in part feeds on the ambiguity of
"their", which comes from the ambiguity of "have" in "the
essences they *have*".

Zeta 7
32^a12. There are several indications that the chapters
Zeta 7-9 make up a separate unit not originally continuous

with Zeta 1-6; for one thing, they are formulated in terms of a full-dress theory of form and matter, which was not at all in evidence in Zeta 4-6 (though in the background in Zeta 5, cf. note); Zeta 10 then resumes the discussion in the terms of "definition" and "essence" that was left off with Zeta 6.

32^{a}15. (i) The Greek of "come-to-be [a-b-c]" is: [*a*] *hypo te tinos gignetai kai* [*b*] *ek tinos kai* [*c*] *ti*.

(ii) Note the ambiguity of "comes-to-be *this*" (*gignetai tode*), as between the coming-to-be of *an individual* (man), and the coming-to-be of something *of this fully determinate constitutive character* or essence (man). The same goes for the idiom rendered "comes-to-be something/somewhat" (*gignetai ti*).

(iii) Hereafter, the following renderings (cf. Glossary) are consistently adhered to as far as possible: *apo* = "from", *ek* = "out of", *hypo* = "by the agency of", ordinary instrumental dative = "by".

32^{a}18. Same as note on 32^{a}15 (ii); is the *ti* the particular man or his *what*?

32^{a}22. A low-key prefiguring of the eventual analysis of the being and coming-to-be of substances in terms of matter's-getting-informed: the *substances* are "capable of being and not-being", in that their *matter* is what is capable of taking the form and of losing it again. Cf. Zeta 15 39^{b}29-30.

32^{a}23. It is not clear whether the "e.g." (*hoion*) attaches to "what comes-to-be" or to "nature"; this translation suggests the latter; if the former is preferred then the version would go, "e.g. a plant, or an animal."

32^{a}24. *hē kata to eidos physis*.

32^{a}28-32. This is *not* the way 'nature' works when things 'come to be from nature' according to the *Generation of Animals*; see Zeta 9 34^{b}6 and note.

32^{a}32. Ross refers to Zeta 7 32^{b}23-30, Zeta 9 34^{a}9-21, ^{b}4-7.

32^{b}5. This lapses into a very loose sense of *ousia* ("substance"), tending toward just "being" (opp. non-being, ab-sence, = *ap-ousia*). On "substance" as having or not having contraries: *Categories* says No (3^b24 ff.); in the presently-rendered portions of the *Metaphysics*, Iota says Yes (cf. Iota 4 with Iota 8). "Contrariety", "possession" and "lack": Iota 3, 4.

32^b21. For 'potentiality' (*dynamis*) and 'potentially' (*dyname*ᵢ), cf. Book Theta.

32^b28. OCT suggestion, 32^b28, a.c. p. 141. Otherwise, reading with Ross, ". . .which is part of the health, or else [follows] by way of more than one step. . .".

32^b30. The analogy between *health* and *house*, and between *warmth* and *stones*, is rather feeble at best; cf. also Ross *AM* ii 184-5.

32^b31. *adynaton genesthai ei mēden pro-hyparkhoi.* "As they say" is wry; the slogan suggests support for Aristotle's view from authorities as divergent from each other as (and as disesteemed by Ar. as) the Eleatics, Empedocles, Anaxagoras and the Atomists.

33^a14. *paragetai xylinos*, i.e., in all but name, the *paronymy* of *Categories* 1^a12-15. *paragōge* is a Hellenistic grammarians' word for "derivation", and Bonitz points out (*Index* 562^b49) that *paragein* = *parōnymiazein* in *Physics* vii 3 254^b11.

33^a23. The explanation here is not yet completely right, for two distinct *ex hou*'s are still imperfectly distinguished. Oversimplifying somewhat:

(1) "The statue is 'out of' the bronze"
is the ('vertical') relation of a thing-with-a-form to its own matter;

(2) "The well (one) is 'out of' the sick (one)"
is the ('horizontal') relation of a thing-with-a-form to an earlier thing-without-that-form (or thing-with-a-lack). (Whether or not the earlier and later things are the *same* thing in this latter case is a separate issue.) The reason why the statue isn't properly called bronze (but may be called

brazen) is *not* the reason why the well (one) isn't properly called sick (but may be called man). At paragraph's end, it is suggested that "comes to be 'out of' " should be restricted to cases of type (2), where the 'out of which' 'doesn't remain' (the type where, e.g., 'the sick (one)' is the 'out of which'); there is nothing against making such a restriction on the expression *ex hou*, but it will not make the type (1) cases go away, and indeed that type is right back with us again at the beginning of Zeta 8, 33^{a}26.

A similar fuzziness of focus on the distinction is found in the famous so-called "introduction of matter" chapter, *Physics* i 7. (Note the evidently unnoticed shift from the second to the first 'out of which' at 190^{a}25). The whole affair seems to be under much better control in Theta 7, *q.v.*

Zeta 8

33^{b}1. *touto hypekeito* can bear either meaning; Ross opts for the "this was assumed", and reads a reference back to ^{a}25 ((b) above) (*AM* ii 187). It seems, though, that the thought, and the surrounding occurrences of *hypokeimenon* and *hypokeisthai* etc. in the meaning of subjecthood, would suggest "this would underlie", "this would be subject"; but that would have to read something like *touto hypokeoito*, of which there is no textual sign.

33^{b}10. Better: "into this he puts it".

33^{b}14. The sentence that follows is a thought-experiment (unsuccessful, it is contended) of "making" the form or essence *sphere*.

33^{b}21. Alternatively: "Or would it never have become a this, if things were so?" Cf. Ross's translation with *AM* ii 189.

33^{b}22. 'This' = *tode*, 'such' = *toionde*.

33^{b}26. Cf. Zeta 10 35^{b}30 and note.

33^{b}32. Cf. Zeta 7 32^{a}24-25, "the nature in respect of the form, which is specifically identical, but in another".

Zeta 9

34ᵃ13. The translation reproduces the inconsequent sentence structure (known as "anacolouthon") of the original.

34ᵃ21. The clause within the stars *. . .* is in the text, but "decidedly suspicious" (Ross) and perhaps should be deleted; *AM* ii 191 34ᵃ20-1 n.

34ᵃ22. Since the product is *homōnymon* with the maker because of being *homo-eides* with it (Zeta 7 32ᵃ24), this use of 'homonym' obviously coincides with the *Categories'* use of 'synonym' (1ᵃ6-12). Cf. note on Zeta 4 30ᵃ34-ᵇ3.

34ᵃ33. *ta physei synistamena*, N.B. *synistanai*, the constitutive process by which individual organisms are formed according to Aristotelian embryology. See below, Zeta 17, note on 41ᵇ30, Eta 3, note on 43ᵇ22.

34ᵇ3. Here the word used is the one for *male* human being: *anēr*, not *anthrōpos*.

34ᵇ6. This surprising remark is not consistent with the official account of animal generation in *GA*; an interesting discussion is given by Peck (*GA*, Loeb ed., pp. 584-6). Cf. above, Zeta 7 32ᵃ28-32.

Zeta 10

34ᵇ31. Acute angle is defined in terms of right angle (as "angle less than a right angle"; cf. 35ᵇ8), finger in terms of man (35ᵇ11).

34ᵇ32. Something is wrong with this last. To be sure, *finger* can't exist without *man* (except homonymously), although the man can without the finger, a familiar claim. It is doubtful however whether the right angle can exist without the acute 'part', whereas the acute seemingly *can* survive, non-homonymously too, its removal from the right. (Cf. Ross *AM* ii 196.) Aristotle may be adverting to the idea that a part's existence within a whole is not "actual", which figures in Zeta 13 39ᵃ3-11, Zeta 16 40ᵇ14 and note.

34^{b}34. "Measure in respect of quantity": cf. Iota 1 52^{b}20-23.

35^{a}5. More accurate would be "*a* matter".

35^{a}9. Alternative version of the parenthesis: "for the form, and the thing *qua* having form, is to be said to be each thing, but the material just in respect of itself, never" (i.e., each thing is to be said to be the form, or the thing *qua* having form).

35^{a}13. Ar. abruptly switches to the dual number (the number "between" singular and plural in Greek, used to refer to exactly two of something), hence apparently he is now thinking not of "segments" in the ordinary sense but of *semicircles* as "segments". See 35^{b}9 below.

35^{a}14. The problem can be put as follows: to what extent is the (kind of) matter left open by the form, and to what is it explicitly required? "Snubness" is not the world's best example of the latter, but it is nonetheless Ar.'s stock one (cf. note on Zeta 5 31^{a}14).

35^{a}23. I.e., the composite. *to syneilēmmenon*, something collected together, that's been (literally) com-pre-hended; from *syllambanein*, to gather up or together. The term *syllabē*, syllable, comes from the same root. (*syllabein* also = to conceive, in the reproductive sense: e.g. *GA* ii 4 739^{a}27.) At Zeta 11 36^{a}27, *ton syneilēmmenon* is used exactly as *ton synolon* has been used in Zeta 10 (35^{a}21, 36^{a}2, cf. 35^{b}22, also 35^{a}6, 35^{b}19, 35^{b}29).

35^{a}32. "Brazen" is not in the text, but is added following a suggestion of Bonitz (and is implied as understood by Alexander's comment).

35^{b}18. I fail to understand this. There are 'works' of the soul that are more fundamental than perception; particularly, the activity of self-sustaining metabolism called *trophē di' hauto* (DA 412^{a}13-16, 413^{a}21-^{b}1), first and fundamental, found without exception in every living thing—plant or animal—on the Earth (413^{a}30-33, ^{b}7-8, 414^{a}32-^{b}1, etc.), and presupposed by all the others. It is true that *to* *aesthētikon* or aisthetic soul is next in the sequence, the most basic of whose diversifications is perception by touch, shared by all animals (413^b4-9); but that does not justify the more global equation suggested by the text. Ross annotates: "And therefore not without soul", which does not help me.

An altogether different possibility is that *aneu aisthēseōs* is "apart from perception" in the sense of "except when perceivable", and the thought is, "each part will be defined in terms of that work which is *seen* as exercised in actuality, though usually latent in potentiality". Cf. Theta 8 50^a16-19. But it is not clear that the Greek will bear this meaning.

35^b30. There are many theories as to the meaning of this. I wonder whether it may not be a way of referring to the *eidos* not as the specific form, but as the species taken collectively, as the population of specified units: "if you wish to think about *the universe determined by Man*, or *Horse*, take this man or horse and generalize him". Thus the 'universal composite' would be in a way the body of the species. Cf. also above, Zeta 8 33^b24-26, and below, Zeta 11 37^a7.

35^b33. "Or [c] of the matter" suppl. Bonitz (received text says simply, "or [b] of the composite 'out of' the form and the matter itself").

36^a7. Cf. Zeta 15 40^a2-5. Alternatively, see note on 35^a18, *fin*.

Zeta 11

36^a26. Note that this is really the same problem as that of Zeta 10. I am inclined to regard Zeta 11 as a subsequent reworking of the Zeta 10 material which if completed would probably have supplanted it (and the Zeta 10 draft would have been discarded).

36^a27. See note on Zeta 10, 35^a23.

36^b13. I have translated as I think it must be meant; the text, however, does *say* something closer to "the formula of two is that of line".Possibly the reference is to Pythagoreans (cf. ^{b}18 below), possibly to Speusippus.

36ᵇ24. "This (form) in that (matter)", *tod' en tōide*; "these (things) holding thus", *hōdi tadi ekhonta*.

36ᵇ25. Socrates the younger's comparison: the one discussed above, comparing flesh/blood : man :: bronze : circle (cf. *AM* ii 203).

36ᵇ30. *ta mere ekhonta pōs*. Right enough, of course, but part of the original question seems to have slipped away: which was whether *man* could exist, not without any 'parts' at all, but without the sorts of parts we're accustomed to (36ᵇ5-7). In *PA* i 1 640ᵃ35 and elsewhere, it is answered, negatively of course.

37ᵃ5. "As was said before," Zeta 10 35ᵃ9, ᵃ31? The paragraph 36ᵇ32-37ᵃ5 doesn't seem to belong here; Alexander et al. think it may have been misplaced from Zeta 10 35ᵃ17; Ross would leave it where it is (*AM* ii 203 f.).

37ᵃ7. The population? *katholou* = collectively? Cf. Zeta 10 35ᵇ30 and note.

37ᵃ10. *houtō* for *te* in line 10 (Apelt).

37ᵃ21. This paragraph is another indication that Zeta 7-9 was interpolated between the surrounding chapters at some time after their original composition; cf. Zeta 7, note on 32ᵃ12.

37ᵃ31. Text continues, "for nose will attach twice over", an obvious interpolation (secl. Ross, *AM* ii 205).

37ᵇ4. I.e., I'm talking about substance = form or essence, rather than substance = the composite. There are evident connections here with Zeta 4 and 6 as regards the '*primary*':

(1) "'primary' means what's not 'something in something *else*' ", cf. Zeta 4 30ᵃ10;

(2) "for things x that are 'primary', x = the Essence of x", cf. Zeta 6 31ᵇ14, 32ᵃ5.

Zeta 12

37ᵇ9. Reference is to *Posterior Analytics* ii 3-10, 13; the aporia is at 92ᵃ29 ff.

37ᵇ12. The term "essence" (*ti ēn einai*) is not used in this chapter, but "that whose formula we call a definition" is standardly essence; cf. note on Zeta 4 29^{b}2. "The Unity of Essence" would thus be an equally appropriate cognomen for Zeta 12 and its follow-up, Eta 6.

37^{b}21.   On "the genus differing", cf. Iota 8.

37^{b}32.   *syllambanomenoi diaphorai*; cf. Zeta 10, note on 35^{a}23.

38^{a}5.   Cf. Zeta 13 38^{b}30-34.

38^{a}11.   What is being described here will hold for many distinct *lines* of specific differentiation within a single genus simultaneously; it should not be regarded as if there were only one. (Though if we were to remain strictly within the "Method of Divisions", as this discussion is pitched to (36^{b}27), the point is doubtful. See *PA* iii 1 643^{b}9 ff., where "Division" has long since been discarded (*PA* i)).

Zeta 13

38^{b}5.   Zeta 3 1029^{a}23 ff.

36^{b}6-8.   The survey of Zeta in the first paragraph of Eta 1 mentions "arguments" purporting to prove that "genus is more substance than the species are, and the universal more than the particulars" (42^{a}12-15).

38^{b}34.   "Obtains apart from them": *khōris hyparkhei autōn*. "Apart from the particulars": *para ta tina*. Cf. Glossary s.v. *para*, *khōris/khōriston*.

39^{a}3.   Literally, "it is clear also thus." But the argument that follows is not against the thesis that "universal is substance", rather it is against a complementary thesis, as indicated by the apposition of the two at 39^{a}14-19 as jointly excluding the 'compositeness' of substance in *any* sense, the paradoxicality of which is then remarked.

39^{a}11.   "Atomic magnitudes", Democritus' *actual* ones and twos.

39^{a}19.   Zeta 1 28^{a}29 ff. Zeta 4 30^{a}22, 29, ^{b}5, 7. Zeta 5 31^{a}13. Etc.

Zeta 14

39ᵃ26-30. This seems very doubtful to me, as it also does at *Cat.* 1ᵃ9-12 and elsewhere where the like is maintained. Possibly in contrast: Iota 8 58ᵃ2-8.

39ᵇ2. Cf. *Parmenides* 131b.

39ᵇ10-11. The clauses within the parenthesis do not cohere very well. The "for" clause suggests the contrast between *kat' allo* and *kath' hauto*, "of another" versus "of itself" or "in respect of itself", familiar from Zeta 4, 6 and 11 (cf. note on Zeta 11 37ᵇ4 for references); the line of thought implied would be, "there will have to be different 'animals' said of each of the different species as their substance, since each such predication is an 'of itself' rather than an 'of another'". But the "were it otherwise" clause apparently picks up on a different line: that man (as a species of animal) is called after no other genus than animal, "otherwise (were it called after something else, then),... etc.". This puts a strained though perhaps not impossible construction on the first clause; but it is the way out that Ross adopts (*AM* ii 213).

Zeta 15

39ᵇ21-22. *syn tēi hylēi syneilēmmenos logos*. Cf. note on Zeta 10 35ᵃ23. The same contrast as here is made in Eta 3, *init*.

39ᵇ25. Cf. note on Zeta 4 29ᵇ14-15.

39ᵇ30. Zeta 7 32ᵃ20-22.

40ᵃ4. (1). Zeta 10 36ᵃ5-9.

40ᵃ4. (2). Or: "the formulae are preserved just the same". The reference of *tōn autōn* is ambiguous.

40ᵃ6. There is some suspicion that something has dropped out of this line; Ross *AM* ii 215, Jaeger OCT 161 n. ("aliquid excidisse vid.").

40ᵃ22. Ross paraphrases: "things which are prior to others are not destroyed when the others are". For "cancelled correspondingly", cf. LSJ⁹, *s.v. ant-an-aireisthai*.

40ᵃ25. = how according to Plato, who says "we are accustomed to posit a single form for every *plurality* of things to which we apply the same name" (*Rep.* x 596ᵃ6-7), Ross's reference, *AM* ii 216.

Zeta 16

40ᵇ9. *pephthē*, lit., "they're *concocted*", as in the metabolic "concocting of residues" among animals, but especially of the catamenia in the course of its getting "worked up" into a fully differentiated 'this'. Cf. *AM* ii 219 40ᵇ9 n. *pettomenon = diorizomenon* ("concocted = defined"), *GA* iv 3 768ᵇ27; *hē thermotēs synkrinei pettousa kai synistēsin* ("the heat, concocting, compounds and integrates"), *GA* iii 11 762ᵇ15.

Ross notes that the "things supposed to be substances", but here denied the title, are just those mentioned in Zeta 2 (28ᵇ8-13) as being popularly regarded as "having the most obvious claim" to it, *AM* ii 218.

40ᵇ10. Or: "something that IS *one*", or: "some one thing".

40ᵇ14. Again a rejection of the idea that full "actualization" or "completedness" can be found below the level of the total organism; cf. the end of this chapter ("no substance consists of substances"), a principle earlier at work also in Zeta 13 39ᵃ3-11, 15-16. Cf. also *PA* i 5 645ᵃ30-36.

40ᵇ16. *symphysei*, which is also the term for "by '*organic*' unity", a somewhat unfortunate ambiguity. Another possibility would be to take *symphysei* not as a contrast to *physei* ("by nature") but as an alternative or even as epexegetic to it: "[either] continuous by nature (but not by force) or by a natural growing-together (for that sort of thing [i.e. merged by force] is a deformity)". But this may reach too far. Cf. Iota 1 52ᵃ22-25.

40ᵇ16-19. Cf. Iota 2 53ᵇ20-28, 54ᵃ13-19.

Zeta 17

41ᵃ9. For a similar suggestion that the study of perceptible substances might be motivated by such a purpose ("getting clear about" immaterial and/or divine substances), cf. Zeta 11 37ᵃ10 ff., and perhaps also the last paragraph of Zeta 3, 29ᵃ33-ᵇ12 (as placed in most modern versions, cf. note on 29ᵇ13).

41ᵃ18. Note that according to the account of the affair that Aristotle recommends, these two questions "why?" elicit fundamentally different answers (sc. the line of thought now under review treats them indifferently).

41ᵃ21. Reading *dia ti anthrōpos esti zōion toiondi* in ᵃ21 (no article before anthrōpos); thus MS Aᵇ. A possible understanding would then be, "why (a) man is such-and-such a kind of animal", but the basic idea of the chapter suggests the reverse. (Why is it a *man*, this sort of animal?)

41ᵃ22. N.B., the question isn't why does *man* attach to *him* (= the man)?

41ᵃ25-26. This looks like something of a shift from Zeta 4 (30ᵃ4, ᵃ11) and Zeta 6 (31ᵇ13), at least of language, but possibly representing a more advanced stage of analysis.

41ᵃ28. Alexander and Jaeger and I think this is a spurious interpolation; Ross defends it (*AM* ii 223). *logikōs*: see Z 4 29ᵇ13.

41ᵇ5. Joachim (according to Ross, *AM* ii 224): why the matter's *there* (*todi*), what it exists *for*. For the textual situation see Ross's a.c.

41ᵇ10-11. Translation and interpretation differ from Ross's, *AM* ii 225. I take this to refer to the type of contextual paraphrase just sketched.

41ᵇ11. Not even the protasis of this sentence (ᵇ11 ff.) is ever completed; the parenthesis beginning "the syllable" is so long that the original construction is forgotten. Cf. Ross's translation, and *AM* ii 225.

41ᵇ13. N.B. the "Unity of Definition" connection (Zeta 12, Eta 6).

41ᵇ22.   There is some MS divergence here; see OCT a.c., p. 165. Here following Ross, *kai eti allou*; on the other popular reading *kai ei ti allo* it would go "this + fire + earth + whatever else, and so on" etc.

41ᵇ30.   *synestēkasi*, another form of *synistanai*, cf. Zeta 9, note on 34ᵃ33.

Eta 1

42ᵃ24.   Note that the foregoing summary pretty well covers the rest of Book Zeta without once mentioning chapters 7-9. Cf. Zeta 7, note on 32ᵃ12.

42ᵃ29.   Form as a 'this', cf. *Meta.* Delta 8 1017ᵇ25; Ross *AM* i 310; notes above on Zeta 7 32ᵃ15, 32ᵃ18.

42ᵃ31.   Forms like e.g. *man* and *shark* are found only as forms enmattered and thus aren't "separate without qualification"; but e.g. the final cause of the celestial motions, the Unmoved Motor, is a form unmattered and hence entirely "separate", cf. e.g. Lambda 7 1073ᵃ3 ff.

42ᵃ32-ᵇ3.   Various difficulties in this paragraph. (1) One is the re-appearance from the *Physics* (or wherever) of the retrograde idea that *anything* "underlying" should underlie as a "matter", regardless of the level of change, seemingly forgetting about the "*two* ways of underlying" doctrine introduced and developed in Zeta 3, 13, 17. See Eta 4 44ᵇ8-11 and note thereon. (It is true that ᵃ34-ᵇ1 only says there is a *subject* for the various nonsubstantial changes, and ᵇ1-3 then says that substantial change goes "similarly" to this with matter as subject; but cf. "topical matter" in the next sentence, 42ᵇ6.) Cf. Theta 8 50ᵇ21-22, on potentiality and matter for "whither-whence", Eta 4 44ᵇ7-8 on matter for *kata topon kinēsis*.

(2) We have to understand a second *ho*, "that which" (i.e., *kai ⟨ho⟩ nun*) in ᵇ2, as indicated, otherwise the text at ᵇ1-3 seems to get the "subjects" of substantial genesis and passing-away wrong. If anything, matter should be subject for both, since that is what survives both; but if "some

'this'" is subject for either, it should be for passing-away—
in Ross's words, "What underlies or undergoes destruction
is matter qualified by a positive form, i.e. a *tode ti*; what
underlies generation is matter qualified by a privation", *AM*
ii 227 ("or undergoes" is the qualifier that makes the interpretation possible). But Ross's attempt to interpret the
Greek as actually *saying* this is unsustainable unless the indicated modification is understood. Otherwise, the text (a)
selects an inappropriate pair with which to make the contrast, and then (b) within that context, gets the contrast
backwards.

42^{b}6. Chief counterexample: planetary bodies, which
move but are indestructible; cf. Eta 4 44^{b}3-8.

42^{b}8. Cf. *Physics* i 7, v 1.

Eta 2

42^{b}9. This instructive chapter is one of Ar.'s more successful attempts at articulating several important themes in
his later thought about substance. It has evident affinities
with e.g. Zeta 17 and Theta 6 and 7, *q.v.*

42^{b}26. (1) Cf. Theta 10 51^{b}9-13, where 'being' = com-
bination, and 'not-being' = separation; see also 43^{a}1 below.

42^{b}26. (2) "it-lies": there is no pronoun ("it") at this
point, the third person form being used. See the next note.

42^{b}25-28. The paraphrases offered (what is really
meant by "a threshold exists", "ice exists", etc.) are as
follows:

(threshold) *to oudos einai* ↔ *to houtōs auto keisthai*
(ice)   *to krystallon einai* ↔ *to houtō*
                                     pepyknōsthai

In the threshold paraphrase, there *does* occur a pronoun
("*its* lying thus," the *auto* in the Greek).

If "threshold" is grammatical subject for "it-lies" in the
first clause of the attempted paraphrase, or antecedent for
"its" (*auto*) in the second, then the would-be analysis is at
best highly misleading, since rendered in this way the

paraphrase fails to bring off—or so much as suggest—the contextual *elimination* of the (pseudo-)substantial term "threshold" that is the aim of the entire enterprise. (The disagreement in gender between *auto* (neuter) and *oudos* (masculine) is not decisive in Aristotle; cf. e.g. *touto* (n.) referring back to *ton desmon* (m.) at Beta 1 995^{a}30-31.)

Alternatively, if *auto* does not refer to the threshold, there are two interpretive possibilities. If in *oudos estin* (42^{b}26), *oudos* is predicate, we then read "a thing is (predicatively) a threshold", and *auto* is that thing. If *oudos* is subject, we understand "there is a threshold", and *auto* is then some un-named subject that underlies the qualification or differentia of position; either way, the intended *analogia* is preserved. In defense of the second way, it may be noted that the over-riding structure of the explication from 42^{b}15 on has been in terms of "things that are said by a composition *of the mat-ter*" (*synthesei legetai tēs hylēs* 42^{b}16), and that this is most likely supposed to be carried through the examples that follow: "by a blending (sc. of the matter)" (*krasei* ^{b}16), . . . , to "by a position (sc. of the matter)" (*thesei* ^{b}19) in the first mention of the threshold case, and so on.

Evidently pseudo-Alexander does not see the (important) issue here: he epitomizes (548.34-37), "So that it's clear that the being and *eidos* of each thing is said in so many ways, for the *eidos* of a threshold and being for a threshold is *auton* be-ing thus placed", and drops the references to the subject matter generally.

In any event, the misstep here, if that is what it is, is redeemed a little further on, when the intended analysis is correctly given (43^{b}7-12).

(In interpreting this passage I have benefited from a clari-fying discussion with John Cooper.)

43^{a}4.   "None of these differentiae" (Ross) is plausible, even likely, from a meaning standpoint, but *ouden* ("none") doesn't agree with *diaphora* ("differentia"). "None of these 'being's", perhaps. The whole clause means something like:

"None of these is substance, (neither in the sense of the substance *of* anything, as is Man), nor 'coupled' (with a matter, as is Man to form Socrates)".

43^{a}7.   Cf. Ross's translation, and his note on 43^{a}4-5 (*AM* ii 229).

43^{a}13.   This means the type of matter involved in the constitution of a particular type of thing, not Socrates' flesh and bones as opposed to Callias'.

Eta 3

43^{a}29.   "A collection of ill-connected remarks on various topics relating to essence and definition"—*AM* ii 231. Scattered, perhaps, but pertinent and informative.

43^{a}31.   For the same contrast cf. Zeta 15 init., 39^{b}20 ff.

43^{a}37.   "Referred to one thing", cf. note on Zeta 4 30^{a}34-^{b}3.

43^{b}4.   I.e. man = Essence of man if "man" means the form (a soul), not if it means the composite.

43^{b}7.   After Bonitz, cf. *AM* ii 321.

43^{b}10.   Not transparent. In this and the next example the idea is that *if* the differentia is taken as another *element* in a substance, part of what it is "composed 'out of' ", *then* something yet further will be required which is not an element, to account for the unity of the whole; the same argument has been used in Zeta 17, and cf. Zeta 8. See the ensuing sentence, and *AM* ii 231-2, 43^{b}11 n.

43^{b}16.   Cf. Zeta 15 39^{b}24-26. For the general perspective, *AM* i 362 f. (Epsilon 3 1027^{a}29 n.), and ii 188 (Zeta 8 33^{b}5 n.).

43^{b}22.   *hosa mē physei synestēken*; recall *synistanai* is one of the technical terms in the embryology for the "compositing" of the animal progeny, each a *systasis* or *systēma*. Cf. Peck's introduction to the Loeb *GA*, p. lxi f. Also above, Zeta 17, note on 41^{b}30, Zeta 9, note on 34^{a}33.

43^{b}32.   I take the idea of this paragraph to be that, as regards the definability of composite *versus* form, the

Antistheneans get it all backwards (on their—misapplied—understanding of the principle that only what is composite can have a formula or 'account').

43^{b}32-44^{a}11. The theme of a connection between "substance" and "number" is resumed in Eta 6 and Iota; see note on Eta 6 45^{a}8.

Eta 4

44^{a}23. Taking *tēn kholēn* as apposite to *eis tēn hylēn*. If instead it is subject of *analyesthai*, then "is 'out of' bile by the bile decomposing into its primary matter".

44^{b}3. With Eta 4 up to this point should be compared Theta 7.

44^{b}8-11. This formulation (44^{b}8-11) is much preferable to (and much more accordant with the "two ways of being subject" line, Zeta 13, than) the formulation that calls that which is "subject" for any change whatsoever, a "matter" for it, as is usual in *Physics, CTBPA*, and even, surprisingly retrograde, right here in *Meta*. Eta above (Eta 1 42^{a}32-^{b}1—see note on 42^{a}32-^{b}3). The spirit of the retort here recommended (to the inquiry about the 'matter' of an eclipse) I take to be, "...*the Moon*. And that's *not* a 'matter' at all, but a perfectly determinate particular individual."

44^{b}15. Sc. and hence succeeds in formulating *what* (the 'form' of) this nonsubstantial entity, the eclipse, *is*. It is hard to see the point of this laboring over the 'formal causes' of nonsubstances, considering that they have just been declared not to have 'material causes' because their subjects are not 'matters' but substantial individuals. As early as Zeta 9 it seemed to be clear that analysis of the 'what it is' of a *non*-substance should *not* be in terms of a form and a matter (though 34^{b}12-16 may also be a falling-off with regard to this).

Eta 5

44^{b}22. See Eta 3, note on 43^{b}16, and the references there.

44^{b}32-34. For the technical contrast of 'possession' and 'lack' (*hexis* and *sterēsis*), cf. Iota 4 55^{a}33-38.

Eta 6
45^{a}8. This is a return to the problem raised in Zeta 12. For the use of *number* as a study object for the "unity" of something that is complex, cf. Eta 3 above, 43^{b}32-44^{a}11, also Iota 1 and 2.

45^{a}11. The context here suggests that "bodies" means the likes of lumps of earth or iron, quantities of water or wine (earth and water are called "simple bodies", iron and wine "compound bodies", e.g. *Physics* ii 1 192^{b}10, *PA* ii 1 646^{a}17, etc.)—not the likes of complex animal bodies and so on. At Delta 4 1014^{b}20-26, "contact" is not identical with or sufficient to produce the sort of organic unity that is in point here. Cf. Lambda 3 1070^{a}10-11 to the same effect. And Zeta 2 28^{b}10 on the 'natural bodies'.

45^{a}13. Zeta 4 30^{b}9-10 made a *contrast* between the "unity" of the Iliad and that of something tied or glued. But there is no "or" in any MS.

45^{a}14. Cf. Zeta 4, note on 30^{a}7-10.

45^{a}33. This is a rather strange statement as it stands; it cannot be meant that it is part of the Essence of sphere that the sphere be actual. The point seems to be that *aside from the maker*, the only other cause of the potential being actual is the essence, which however is the essence of both. (I owe this interpretation to Nicholas White, who refers to 45^{b}21-22. As he puts it: "Well, but he's left aside the maker. And the point is that once you do *that*, the *ti ēn einai* is all you have, there isn't any more!")

45^{b}10. MSS, Alexander and William of Moerbeke's Latin translation (13th c.) all have *synousian psychēs*, "communion of psyche"; Ross deletes *psychēs* "of psyche" as an intrusion from the following line (*AM* ii 239).

45^{b}20. "An obviously absurd question"—*AM* ii 239. I cannot imagine why Ross says this; the "causes of unity" are

Aristotle's central metaphysical preoccupation, and the connections of unity and being a repeated theme.

Theta 1

45ᵇ27. General note on Theta. Not least of the difficulties in rendering this book of the *Metaphysics* is that of rendering *dynamis*, whose meanings range over all of: power, potency, potentiality, ability, capability, capacity, faculty, possibility. Likewise *dynaton*: potent, potential, able, capable, possible. *dynameᵢ*, the dative of the noun, used adverbially, can almost always be given as "potentially". In the Eek version of Theta, the words *dynamis*, *dynaton*, *dynameᵢ*, *energeia* (here usually "actuality" or "actualization") and *entelekheia* ("completedness") were simply transliterated, in hopes that some sort of "definition in use" would materialize; however, none did; and the version was too close to unintelligible to remain in that form. Thus here these terms have been rendered variously as the context seems to require, a compromise of the strictest standards of Eeking; but at least the many-oneness of the Eek-to-Greek relation entails that the single original is always recoverable.

45ᵇ33. The MSS have *ti* accented acute, to mean "what"; interpreters quarrel over whether it should be left so (e.g. Bonitz), or accented grave, to mean "a certain", "a particular" (e.g. Ross). Cf. Zeta 7, notes on 32ᵃ15, 32ᵃ18.

46ᵃ6. "Homonymously": cf. note on Zeta 4, 30ᵃ34-ᵇ3.

46ᵃ28. *sympephyken*: a buzzword; cf. Zeta 16, note on 40ᵇ15.

46ᵃ35. *esterēsthai*, "are lacking", "have been deprived": cf. Theta 2 46ᵇ13-15, Iota 4 55ᵇ3-9, ᵇ21-22.

Theta 2

46ᵇ11-12. The text has twice *kath' hautas*: *tou men kath' hautas tou de mē kath' hautas*, where "in" ("not in") "respect of themselves" has to refer to the knowledges; the

translation follows this. But twice *kath' hauto* would make
better sense, "in" ("not in") "respect of itself" referring to
each of the contraries—as in the next line. ^{b}10-12 would then
go: "thus it's necessary that these sorts of knowledges also
be of their contraries, but of the one [contrary] in respect of
itself and of the other not in respect of itself".

46^{b}23. Dropping the words *tois aneu logou dynatois*,
which are as Ross observes "rather pointless" (*AM* ii 243).

Theta 3
46^{b}29-30. "A thing is capable [of acting] only when it
is acting": *hotan energēi monon dynasthai*. "When it's not
acting it's not capable of acting": *hotan de mē energēi ou
dynasthai*.

47^{a}24-26. Ross, *AM* ii 245: "Considered as a definition of *dynaton*, this statement would evidently be circular
and therefore worthless. But it does not claim to be a definition. It only amounts to saying that before you can pro-
nounce anything to be possible, you should satisfy yourself
that none of its consequences is impossible. It is a criterion
for the determination of possibility in doubtful cases."

However, it seems to be closer to a definition than Ross
allows. Cf. *APr* i 13 32^{a}18-20: "I say *being possible* and *the
possible* of that which, not being necessary, but being supposed to belong, nothing impossible will come about
through this". Whether or not Aristotle thinks it a definition, it is an important modal principle; stated in proposi-
tional form (rather than the predicative form that is suggested by "belongs"):

"if *p* is possible, then if *p* is, nothing impossible follows"
or

$$\Diamond p \rightarrow \sim [(p \rightarrow q) \mathrel{\&} \sim \Diamond q].$$

Cf. note on Theta 4, 47^{b}14-16.

47^{a}30-31. For the connection, see Theta 6 48^{b}18-35,
Theta 8 50^{a}21-23.

Theta 4

47^{b}3 (1). *akolouthei*, "accompanies" in the sense "is compatible with", rather than "logically follows from", for which the normal word is *symbainei*, as 47^{b}19, 49^{a}36 below. Cf. *de Int*. 12-13.

47^{b}3 (2). An emendation proposed by Zeller would alter the reading to: "If, as has been said, that is possible which does not lead to any impossibility, evidently. . .etc." It has the merit of linking the principle of Theta 3 47^{a}24-26 more explicitly with the argument that follows, which uses that principle. On the other hand there is no *textual* question about the text. See *AM* ii 147.

47^{b}6. "The things that cannot be would vanish". Sc. "If it is true that a thing is possible but will never be, then anything is possible, and then nothing is impossible".

47^{b}7. "Be measured" in this paragraph means "measured as commensurate with the side", and thus amounts to "be commensurate".

47^{b}14-16. The principle here stated and then argued is:
$$(p \rightarrow q) \rightarrow (\Diamond p \rightarrow \Diamond q).$$
It is in fact logically equivalent to that at Theta 3 47^{a}24-26; see note.

Theta 6

48^{b}23-24. The words for "and has seen", "and has understood" are supplied in the text by Ross, following Bonitz' conjecture, on analogy with those for "and has thought" (which are in the MSS), and other parallels. The insertion is defended at *AM* ii 251-2.

48^{b}25. It is of some importance in the understanding of the distinction being propounded in this passage, to know that the difference between "I am X-ing" and "I have X-ed" in ancient Greek, i.e. between the 'kinetic' and 'stative' forms of the verb, is not primarily a difference of *tense* between present and past, but a difference of what linguists call *Aktionsart* or *Behandlungsart*: "*I have seen*", for example, does not mean "I saw (in the past)", but "*I am (presently) in the state of having completed (i.e. 'perfected') an act of seeing*". It is in these terms that the *telos* of house-building, having-house-built, which means having finished the house, could not have started to 'be' while the house-building was still going on, and once the *telos* has started to 'be' entails that the house-building must have stopped; whereas having-seen 'is' at every moment when the seeing 'is'.

("Has he *finished* (a) housebuilding?"—appropriate;
(b) seeing?"—inappropriate.)

(There is some terminological variation extant as between the language of *Aktionsart* and of *aspect*; see O. Szemerényi, *Einführung in die vergleichende Sprachwissenschaft* (2nd ed., Darmstadt, 1980), pp. 286-288, 310.

48^{b}28.   The word for "should be" is supplied by Ross, again following Bonitz.

48^{b}33.   The words for "as are moving and having moved" are deleted by Jaeger.

48^{b}35.   Ar. might have remarked here, but in fact postpones remarking until Theta 8 50^{a}21, that the word *energeia* itself is a compound, *ergon* (work or function), *en* (in): *energeia* is something whose work or function is *internal* to it. The word *en-telekheia* is constructed in the same way: something whose *telos* (completion or end) is *within*. Thus 48^{b}22-23, "in which its completion is contained", and see note to 48^{b}25, also *AM* ii 246 (Theta 3 47^{a}30 n.). (An alternative interpretation would reconstruct *en-ergeia* as "in action" or "in actuality", and *en-telekheia* as "in a state of completion". This would parallel 48^{b}20, "are in movement".)

Theta 7

49^{a}1-3.   A loose illustration, of course: Ar. does not regard semen as matter for the offspring, or "potentially man" in that sense: cf. e.g. *GA* i 21 729^{a}34 ff. etc.

49ª14. *di' autou* Ross following MS A^b and Alexander, *di' hautou* MSS EJ.

49ª15. *pesein* ("cast") is Ross's addition; otherwise "it needs to be in another". It would be tempting to regard this as an effort at improving on the earlier misstatement about the causal role of semen (cf. note on 49ª1-3), but unfortunately Ar. immediately equates this case with one of earth's metamorphosing into bronze. Ross is very probably correct in commenting: "he writes as if he accepted the popular view which treated the male and female elements as uniting to form the matter of offspring. He is merely illustrating a general principle, and in such cases he often writes from the point of view of a common theory not his own", *AM* ii 255.

49ª18. Cf. Zeta 7 33ª5-end.

49ª27. "Fire is prime": as just specified by ª24-26, fire is here "prime" on the stipulation that there is nothing *X* lying beneath (= "subject to") it with respect to which fire is *X*-en.

49ª28. Apelt's reading, *to kath' hou*, is plainly required (as against *to katholou* of the codices and Alexander; cf. *AM* ii 257). The ensuing paragraph enlarges on "the matter's not being a 'this'", ª27.

Theta 8
49ᵇ34. "The sophistical elenchus": see e.g. *Euthydemus* 275-7.

50ª14. For the textual problem, *AM* ii 262-3.

50ª20. "The Hermes of Pauson": apparently a trick painting in which it was difficult to tell what was within and what outside the picture; the ancient explicative attempts make little sense. *AM* ii 263-4.

50ᵇ24. *peri physeōs*, traditional title of Empedocles's physics-poem.

Theta 10

51^{b}32. *noein*, "think", in this context has the force of "know"; and at the end of the next paragraph (52^{a}3) *noētikon*, "thinking faculty" could be "cognitive faculty".

Iota 1

52^{a}15. "One", "that which is one", "a unit": the Greek word fluctuates in this discussion among all of these meanings; some such shifts are signalled in subsequent notes. The word is *hen* unless otherwise indicated.

52^{a}18. *prōtōn* ("primary") MSS, Ross, *prōtōs* ("primarily") Sylburg, OCT.

52^{a}22-25. It is impossible to pin down the reference of *toiouton* ("of this sort") and *hosa* ("such things as are") with any confidence in these lines; the bracketed suggestions are guesses. Alternatively, it could be hazarded that "has in itself the cause of itself being *continuous*" at ^{a}24-25 implies that *toiouton* means "continuous" throughout.

52^{a}24. There is an evident reference here to Eta 2 42^{b}16-18 (cf. also Zeta 16, note to 40^{b}16, and Delta 6 1015^{b}36-1016^{a}1).

52^{b}3. From here to 52^{b}19, the focus shifts in the direction of 'unit' in the sense of 'unit measure', whose source (*enteuthen*, "whence") is said to be in quantity (q.v. below).

52^{b}5-7. Commentators call this an introduction of a connotation/denotation distinction. But it is late in the day for such metalanguage here; the Socratic-dialogue terminology of definition versus examples would do.

52^{b}16. For 'being F_d' see note to Zeta 4 29^{b}14-15.

52^{b}27. I.e., the contraries heavy/light, fast/slow (see the explanation).

53^{a}18. Omitting *kai hē pleura* in ^{a}18. The meaning seems to be, the diagonal is measured as one part equal to the side, and another part incommensurable with the side.

53ª24. 53ª5 above; cf. Delta 6 1016ª17-24.

53ª35. Following Ross's text, which has *hēmōn* "of us". MS A^b and Alexander have *hēmin* "to us", which would result in something like "the cubit-rule's applying to us so-and-so much".

Iota 2
53^b10. Beta 4 1001ª4-^b25 ("Eleventh Aporia").

53^b11. For the textual problem at ^b11, see *AM* ii 285, OCT a.c. p. 198.

53^b16. Empedocles, Anaximenes, Anaximander.

53^b17. Zeta 13, 16.

Iota 3
54ª31. This work seems not to be extant; a book "On Contraries" is mentioned in Diogenes Laertius' catalogue (5.22). Cf. *AM* i 259 (Gamma 2, 1004ª2 n.).

54^b13. Ross's text; see *AM* ii 287-8.

54^b15. This and the next occurrence of "other" translate *allo* rather than *heteron*. I see no significance in the variation.

54^b15-16. See note on 54^b22.

54^b18. See "same" (sense 3) above, 54ª35-^b3.

54^b22. Both here at ^b22 and earlier at 54^b15-16 it is a mistake to translate with Ross "one or not one with anything *else*" (earlier, "the same as or other than everything *else*"); there is no such word in the text and the argument requires that the variables be interpreted nonexclusively.

54^b23. *diaphora kai heterotēs allo* (cf. note on 54^b15).

54^b29-30. Presumably, things belonging to different maxima genera = categories. Cf. "column of predication" just below, and Iota 8 58ª13.

55ª2. Delta 9, 28. See Iota 4.

Iota 4
55ª26. The likely reference is to ª6 above; but this does not square well with e.g. Iota 3 54^b27-30, 35. See note on Iota 7, 57^b20.

55ª31-33. Punctuation follows Ross's tr., not Ross's text.

55ᵇ7. Delta 22.

55ᵇ8. "Associated with the recipient", i.e. implies that the subject could possess the positive predicate, "determinate", i.e., limited to such a subject. (Ross, *AM* ii 292, 55ᵇ4 n.)

55ᵇ13-15. I render this as the sense seems to require, though the Greek looks more like the converse, and the parenthetical "the reason being" could go with the converse. White most helpfully proposes emending the text, reversing *sterēsis/enantiōsis* and *enantiotēs/sterēsis*. (The text looks pretty careless in any case, since it has "contrariety" where it should have "contrary"; cf. ᵇ18, "every contrariety has a lack as one of its contraries".)

55ᵇ18. Reading *thateron* with Alexander and Ross. MSS E, J, Gamma: *thaterou*, "every contrariety has a lack *of* one of its contraries" (?).

55ᵇ21. Cf. 55ᵇ3-7 above.

Iota 5

56ª10-11. A Platonic theory; Nu 1 1087ᵇ7.

56ª14. Iota 4 55ª16.

56ᵇ1. In the technical sense of Iota 4 55ª6, 26.

Iota 6

56ᵇ21. Lit. stative "action-type", "the things in a present state of having been measured". Cf. Theta 6, note on 48ᵇ25.

56ᵇ31. [Some nerve, what?!!]

56ᵇ35. Delta 15 1021ª26-30.

Iota 7

57ᵇ8-9. An allusion to the *Timaeus*, 67d-e; "separative" and "compositive".

57ᵇ20. More uncertainty as to contraries' being possibly extrageneric or not; this conflicts with 57ª28-30 above, Iota 8 58ª10-11 below. Cf. Iota 4, note on 55ª26.

Iota 8

57^{b}35. *tinos ti heteron*, "other than something [and] another something" i.e., as I read it, *heteron tinos kai heteron ti*; the idiom is slightly different from that of Iota 3 54^{b}26, *tinos tini diaphoron*. It is hard to render; David Blank has suggested "[a thing] other than a[nother] thing", which conveys the desperateness of the difficulty. (For *heteron ti* as "something else", cf. Zeta 17 41^{b}17, 19.) Ross treats the *ti* here as an "accusative of respect" and translates the two phrases identically (*AM* ii 301); but there may be more to it than that. See note on Zeta 7 32^{a}15.

58^{a}2-5.   See note on Zeta 14 39^{a}26-30.

58^{a}11.   Iota 4, 55^{a}16; cf. Iota 7, note on 57^{b}20. It should be noted that "differentia" and "difference" render the same Greek word, *diaphora*.

58^{b}13.   Iota 3 54^{b}35, note on 54^{b}29-30.

Iota 9

58^{a}30-31.   "The difference a contrariety": in Iota 3 and 4, contrariety has been characterized as a species of difference rather than, as suggested here, the other way round (contrariety as "a certain difference" 54^{b}32, "greatest difference" 55^{a}4-5, "complete difference" 55^{a}16), and the logic of the aporia points in the same direction. However, I leave it.

58^{b}5.   "Single word", such as 'cloak' for 'pale man' in Zeta 4, or for 'rounded bronze' in Eta 6.

Iota 10

58^{b}29.   It seems plain that *genos* and *eidos* must bear a non-technical sense in this chapter, since such claims as this would be seriously inconsistent with the foregoing if rendered "genus" and "species". See *AM* ii 305.

58^{b}34.   I depart slightly from Ross's punctuation to follow the (clear) sense.

Glossary

Note: Z = Zeta, H = Eta, T = Theta, I = Iota.

I. Greek to Eek

αἴσθησις, *aisthēsis* perception Z10 35b18; Z15, T5, I1, 3
 ἀισθητόν, *aisthēton* perceptible Z2 28b18; Z8, 10-11, 14-17, H1-3, 6, T3
αἴτιον, *aition* cause Z8 33b26; Z9, 13, 16-17, H1-2, 4, 6, I1
ἀπλοῦν, *haploun* simple Z4 30a16; Z5, Z17, H1 42a8 (simple bodies), I1
 ἀπλῶς, *haplōs simpliciter* Z1 28a31; Z4-5, 7, 10-11, Z17, H1, 6, T6-8, I1, 3, 6
 absolutely Z12 38a5; 14, 7
 completely I3 54b12
ἀπό, *apo* from Z7 32a13, 27
 apo tautomatou spontaneously Z7 32a13; Z8, 9
ἀπορεῖν, *aporein* be in aporia, be puzzled Z1 28b3; Z10-11, H6 (**NOTE** Z 1 28a20)
 ἀπορία, *aporia* aporia Z5; Z11-13, H3, 5-6, I2
 ousia aporōtatē substance most puzzling Z3 29a33
 tis aporēseien someone might get in difficulties Z1 28a20; Z9, I5-6, 9
ἄρχειν, *arkhein* start, start off, begin Z2 28b22; Z7, 9
 ἀρχή, *arkhē* first principle Z2 28b22; Z13, 17, H1, T8
 starting-point Z7 32b16; Z9
 origin Z10 35a24; Z13, 16, H1, T1-2, 7-9, I1, 7
γεννᾶν, *gennan* generate Z7 32a25; Z8, 15, H3
γένος, *genos* genus Z3 28b35; Z4, 7-8, 12, 14-15, H1-2, T8, I1-9
 kind H2, I10

γίγνεσθαι, *gignesthai* come-to-be Z7-10, H3, 5, T6, 8, 10, I2-3, 8 (**NOTE** Z 7 32a15)
become, come about T7 49a2
γένεσις, *genesis* coming-to-be Z7 32a16; Z8-9, 13, 15, 17, H1, 3-6, T3, 8, 14
γιγνόμενα,. *gignomena* things that come-to-be Z7 32a12; Z8, H5, T8, I4
γνῶναι, *gnōnai* know Z1 28a37, 28b2; Z3, 6, T9, I1
γνωρίζειν, *gnōrizein* know, recognize Z 10 36a8, Z15, 16
γνῶσις, *gnōsis* knowledge Z1 28a33; T8
γνωστόν, *gnōston* known I1 52a32
διαφέρειν, *diapherein* differ Z12 37b21; I4, 8, 9
διαφορά, *diaphora* difference, differentia Z12 37b19; Z15, H2, 6, I3-5, 7-9
δύνασθαι, *dynasthai* be able, be possible (**NOTES** Theta 1 45b27, Theta 3 47a24-26)
δύναμις, *dynamis* potentiality, power, *et al.* Z3 29a13; Z7-8, Z16, T 1 (45^{b}33), T *passim*, I4
δυνάμει, *dynamei* potentially Z7 32b21; Z9, 13, 16, H1-2, 5-6
δυνατόν, *dynaton* potential *et al.* T *passim*
ἀδυναμία, *adynamia, to adynatein* incapacity Z12 38a13; T1, I4, 10
εἰδέναι, *eidenai* know Z1 28a36, 28b1; Z16
εἶδος, *eidos* (Pl.) form Z2 28b20; Z6, 8, 11, 14, 16, H1, I10
εἶδος, *eidos* (Ar.) form (vs. matter), species (vs. genus) Z3 29a6; Z7-12, 17, H1-6, T8, I1, 3-4, 7-10
εἶναι, *einai* to be, being Z3 29a22
εἶναι μουσικῷ, *einai mousikōi* being musical$_d$, essence of musical Z4 29b14; Z6, 15-17, H3, I1-2 (**NOTE** Zeta 4 29b14-15)
ὄν, τό, *on, to* that which is, being Z1 28a10 (**NOTE** Z1, 28a10)
οὐσία, *ousia* substance Z1 28a15; Z2-14, 16-17, H1-4, T1, 7-8, I1-3, 10

ἐκ, *ek* out of Z2 28b12; Z3-5, 7-17, H1, 3-5, T8, 10, I1-4, 6-7 (**NOTE** Z7 33a23)

ἔλεγχος σοφιστικός, *elenkhos sophistikos* sophistical elenchus Z6 32a6, T8

ἕν, μονάς, *hen, monas* one, unit Z2 28b17; Z4, 6, 8, 12, 15-17, H3, 6, I1-6

ἐναντίωσις, *enantiōsis* contrariety I3 54b32; I4, 6, 8-9
    ἐναντίον, *enantion, enantia* contrary, contraries Z7 32b2; Z12, 14, H5, T1-2, 5, 9-10, I1, 3-10

ἕνεκα οὗ, *heneka hou* purpose, "for the sake of which" Z17 41a29; H4, T8

ἐντελέχεια, *entelekheia* completedness (cf. telos) Z10 36a6; Z13, H3, 6, T1, 3, 8
    ἐντελεχείᾳ, *entelekheia*ᵢ in completedness Z9 34b17; Z13, Z16, T7

ἐπιστήμη, *epistēmē* (*epistēton, epistēmikon*) knowledge, understanding Z4 30a33; Z6, 7, 15, H6, T2, 8, I1, 4, 6-7

ἕξις, *hexis* disposition, possession, tendency H5 44b32; T1, I4-5

ἔργον, *ergon* work, function (**NOTE** T6 48a35)
    ἐνέργεια, *energeia* actuality, actualization H2 42b10; H3, 6, T1, 3, 6, 8, 9
    ἐνεργείᾳ, *energeia*ᵢ actually H1 42a28; H6, T6, 8, 10
    ἐνεργεῖν, *energein* act, become active, be active T3 46b29; T8, 10

ᾗ, *hēi qua* Z10 35a8, Z12 38a12; T1, 8, I1, 9

ἰδέα, *idea* idea (Pl.) Z6 31a31; Z11, 14, 15, H1, T8

ἴδιον, *idion* peculiar, unique Z9 34b16; H4
    co-extensive Z13 38b10, 23
    (*idia*ᵢ, from their own viewpoint) H1 42a7, 11

κατά, *kata* in respect of, according to, *et al.* Z1 ff.
    κατὰ συμβεβηκός, *kata symbebēkos per accidens* Z3 29a26; Z4-6, 8-9, 12, 14, H5, T2, 10, 17, 9-10
    καθ' αὑτό, *kath' hauto* in respect of itself Z1 28a23; Z4-6, Z8-11, 14, H1, T2, I1, 7-9 (**NOTE** Z 4 29b15)
    in its own right Z3 29a20; of itself T8

καθ'ἕκαστον, *kath' hekaston* particular, singular Z1
28a27; Z10, 11, 15, 16, H1, I1, 10
καθ'ἕν, *kath' hen* in respect of one thing Z4 30b3
καθ'ὅ, *kath' ho* in respect of which Z7 32a22
καθ'οὗ, *kath' hou* that of which Z3 28b36, T7
καθόλου, *katholou* universal Z3 28b34; Z10, 11, 13, 16, H1,
I2, 10
κατηγορεῖσθαι, *kategoreisthai* be predicated Z1 28a13;
Z3, 13, 15, H2 (**NOTE** Z1 28a10[2])
κατηγορία, *kategoria* category, thing-predicated Z5
31a2; Z9, T1, 3, 10
κατηγόρημα, *kategorema* thing-predicated Z1
28a33, I2
κατηγορούμενον, *kategoroumenon* thing-predicated
Z1 28a13; Z4
κινεῖν, *kinein* move, produce movement H4 44a28 (*kin-
ousa*); T2, 5-6, 8
κίνησις, *kinesis* motion, movement Z4 29b25; Z7, 9,
11, 16
κινητικόν, *kinetikon* movemental T8 49b7
κινητή, *kinete* changeable Z10 36a10
λέγειν, *legein* say, formulate Z4 29b20; Z5, 12, 15, 17, H3,
6
λέγεσθαι, *legesthai* be said, be called Z1 28a10; Z3,
13, H2, I3 (**NOTE** Z 1 28a10)
λεγόμενον, *legomenon* what is said, thing said H3
λόγος, *logos* formula, argument Z1, Z4, 5, Z6 31b18,
7 ("account"), 9-15, 17, H1-4, 6, T1-2, 3 ("theory"), 5
("reason"), 8, I1, 9
λόγῳ, *logo$_i$* in formula Z1 28a32; Z10, 13, 15, H1, T8,
I3
λογικῶς, *logikos* by a formula, from its formula Z4
29b13; Z17
μαθημάτικα, *mathematika* mathematika (Pl., cf. *Rep.* vi)
Z2 28b20, H1
(mathematics) Z11 36b32 ff

μεταβολή, *metabolē* change H1 42a33; H5, T1-2, T8, I4
    μεταβλητικόν, *metablētikon* of change T1 46a15; T8
    μεταβάλλειν, *metaballein* to change Z7 33a21, T7, I7
μετέχειν, *metekhein, methexis, metokhē* participation Z4
    30a13, Z6, 11, 14, 15, H6
μορφή, *morphē* shape Z3 29a3; Z8, H1-3, 6, I1
νόησις, *noēsis* thinking Z7 32b15; T9, I1
    νοητόν, *noēton* intelligible Z10 36a3; Z11, H3, 6
    νοεῖν, *noein* to think, reason Z7 32b6, T10
οἰκεῖον, *oikeion* proper Z 12 38a24; H4, I9
ὁμώνυμον, *homōnymon, homōnymōs* homonym, homo-
    nymously Z4 30a32; Z9, 10, T1, 10
ὅπερ, *hoper* hoper Z4 30a3; H6, T10, I1 (**NOTE** Z4
    30a2-7)
ὁρίζειν, *horizein* determine, define Z4 29b1; Z10, 11, Z15,
    H1, 3, 6
    ὡρισμένον, *hōrismenon* determinate Z1 28a27; Z8
    33b22, T8 49b6, I4
    ὥρισται, *hōristai* is demarcated Z3 29a21
    ὁριζόμενον, *horizomenon* demarcated Z3 29a18; Z10
    ὁρισμός, *horismos* definition Z4 30a7, Z5, 10-12, 15,
    H1-2, 6, T1 (**NOTES** Z 4 29b2, 29b20)
    ὅρος, *horos* definition Z5 30a8
    διορίζειν, *diorizein* determine Z3 29a1; Z11 37a14,
    Z17, T1, T6-8, I4
    prosdiorizesthai T5 48a17
    diorismenon I10 58b27
    diorismos T5 48a2, 20
οὐρανος, *ouranos* universe, heaven Z2 28b12; H1 42a10,
    T8 50b23
παρά, *para* beyond, besides, apart from, over and above
    Z2 28b18; Z6, 8, 11-16, H1, H6, T8, I2
    (force of *para* close to that of *khōris*: Z13 38b30-34,
    Z16 40b27, and to *khoriston*: Z15 40a18-20, H6 45b7)
πάσχειν, *paskhein* be affected, be afflicted, suffer, be
    acted upon, undergo Z12 37b16; H4, T1, 5, I9

πάθος, *pathos* affliction Z1 28a19; Z3-5, 13, H1, 4, 6, T7, I2-3, 9

παθητικόν, *pathētikon* affective, affectible T1 46a13, T5

πλῆθος, *plēthos* plurality I1 53a30; I3, 6

ποίησις, *poiēsis* making, producing Z7 32a27; Z8, H3, 6, T2, 8, I4

ποιόν, ποσόν, *poion, poson* so-qualified, so-much; quality, quantity Z1 28a12; Z3, 4, 7, 9, 10, 13, H6, T1, 8, I1

πολλαχῶς, *pollakhōs* in many ways Z1 28a10; Z5, 10, T1, I1, 3-4

πλεοναχῶς, *pleonakhōs* in several ways, more than one way Z4 30a18; H4

ποσαχῶς, *posakhōs* the number of ways Z1 28a11; T8, I1

πρός, *pros* in reference to, referred to Z4

πρὸς ἕν, *pros hen* referred to one thing Z4 30a35; H3 (**NOTE** Z4 30a34-b3)

πρῶτον, *prōton* primary, first Z1 28a14; Z3, 4, 6, 7, 9, 11, 17, H3-5, T1-2, 7-8, I1, 3-4, 7 (**NOTE** Z11 37b4)

πρώτως, *prōtōs* primarily Z1 28a30; Z4, 10, T1, I1, 10

πρότερον, *proteron* prior Z3 29a6; Z6, 10, 12, 13, 15, T1, 7 ("sooner"), 8, I7

ὕστερον, *hysteron* posterior Z3 29a31; Z10, 12, T8-9

σπέρμα, *sperma* seed Z7 32a31, T8

στέρησις, *sterēsis* lack Z7 32b3; Z8, H1, 4-5, T1, 2, I2-5, 10

deprivation H4 44b14

ἐστερῆται, *esterētai* is lacking T1 46a35; T2, I4, 6

στοιχεῖον, *stoikheion* (phonetic) element Z10 34b26; Z12, 16, 17, H1, 3, I1

συλλαμβάνειν, *syllambanein* take together, incorporate, combine Z12 37b31 (**NOTE** Z 10 35a23)

συλλαβή, *syllabē* syllable Z10 34b26; Z17

συνειλήμμενον, *syneilēmmenon* taken together, composited Z10 35a23; Z11 36a27, Z15, I9

"associated" I4 55b8

συνείληπται, *syneilēptai* Z10 35a34

συμβαίνειν, *symbainein* follow Z6 31a26; Z7, 11, 13, 14, I5

συνδεδυάσμενον, *syndedyasmenon*, *syndyazomenon* coupled Z5 30b16, 31a6; H2 43a4 (**NOTE** Z5 31a14)

συνδέσμῳ, *syndesmō*$_i$ by being tied together Z4 30b9, H6

σύνθεσις, *synthesis* composition Z13 39a12; H2, 6

σύνθετον, *syntheton* compound Z4 29b23, Z13, 15, 17, H3, T10, I7 (**NOTE** on Z3 29a5)

(has degrees: "less compounded" Z 15 40a23)

ἀσύνθετον, *asyntheton* non-composite T10 51b17, 19

συνίστανaι, *synistanai* be composited Z17 41b30, H3 (**NOTE** Z9 34a33)

συνιστάμενα, *synistamena* composited Z9 34a33

σύνολον, *synolon* composite Z3 29a5, Z8, 10, 11, 15, 19 (**NOTE** on Z 3 29a5)

σχῆμα, *skhēma* configuration Z3 29a4, Z7

'figure' H6 45a35; I2 54a3; of Categories T10, I3

σωρός, *sōros* heap Z16 40b9; Z17, H3, H6

τέλος, *telos* completion H1 42a4; H4, T6, 8-9, I4

τέλειον, *teleion* complete T6, I4

τελευταῖον, *teleutaion* completing Z7 32b17; Z12 (*entelekheia, q.v.*) completedness

τέχνη, *tekhnē* art Z7 32a18; Z8, 9, H4, T2

τί ἐστι, *ti esti* what it is Z1 28a11, Z4, 7, 9, H2-3, T1, 10, I1-2

τί ἦν εἶναι, *ti ēn einai* essence Z3 28b34; 4-8, 10, 11, 13, 17, H1, 3, 6 (**NOTES** Z4 29b2, Z6 32a11)

τόδε τι, *tode ti* a this, some this Z1 28a12; Z3, 4, 8, 11-14, H1, 3, 6, T7

ὕλη, *hylē* matter Z3 29a2; Z7-11, 15-17, H1-6, T6-8, I3-4, 8-9 (**NOTE** Z7 32a22)

ὑπάρχειν, *hyparkhein* belong Z2 28b8; Z3-6, 13, 16, 17,
T2, 6, 8, I8, 10
obtain Z13 38b32
apply Z6 31b4, Z15 40a15
occur Z16 40b26, 27
be present Z7 32b7, T5 48a12, T8
50b22, T10 51b21
ὑπό, *hypo* by the agency of Z3 29a18; Z7-9, T1, 8, "under"
I4 55a31
ὑποκεῖσθαι, *hypokeisthai* is subject, underlies Z13 38b5;
I2
ὑποκείμενον, *hypokeimenon* subject Z1 28b26; Z3,
4, 6, 8, 11, 13, 15, H1-2, T7, I1, 4-5 (**NOTE** Z3 28b35-36)
substrate Z7 33a8, Z8
φθείρεσθαι, *phtheiresthai* cease-to-be, be destroyed Z10
35a25; Z15, H3, T1, 10
φθορά, *phthora* ceasing-to-be, passing-away, destruction Z15 39b23, Z17, H1, 4
corruption H5
φθαρτόν, *phtharton* destructible H3 43b15; I10
φύσις, *physis* nature Z2 28b25; Z6-8, 15, 17, H3, 5, T8,
I1-2, 8
φύσει, *physei* by nature Z7 32a12; Z9, 16, 17, H4, T1,
9, I1
φυσικόν, *physikon* natural Z2 28b10; Z7-8, H1, 4
χρόνῳ, *khronō*ᵢ in time Z1 28b33, Z13, T8
χωρίζεσθαι, *khōrizesthai* be separated Z1 28a23; Z10, 11,
Z16 40b7, 28
exist separately T6 48b17
κεχωρισμένον, *kekhōrismenon* (having been) separated Z14 39b31, Z 16 40b7, Z17
χωρίς, *khōris* apart (from) Z5 30b25, Z13-16 (cf. s.v.
para)
χωριστόν, *khōriston* separate (adj.) Z1 28a34; Z3,
13-15, H1, 6, I1-2
independent T6 48b15
ψυχή, *psykhē* soul Z2 28b23; Z7, 16

II. Eek to Greek

able, be *dynasthai*
absolutely *haplōs*
account *logos*
act, become active *energein*
acted upon, be *paskhein*
actuality, actualization *energeia*
affected, be *paskhein*
affective, affectible *pathētikon*
affliction *pathos*
apart from *para, khōris*
aporia *aporia*
apply *hyparkhein*
argument *logos*
art *tekhnē*

become *gignesthai*
begin *arkhein*
belong *hyparkhein*
besides, beyond *para*
by agency of *hypo*

called, be *legesthai*
category *katēgoria*
cause *aition*
cease-to-be *phtheiresthai*
ceasing-to-be *phthora*
change *metabolē* (n.), *metaballein* (v.)
changeable *kinētē*
co-extensive *idion*
combine *syllambanein*
come-to-be, come about *gignesthai*
coming-to-be *genesis*
complete *teleion*
completedness *entelekheia*

completely   *haplōs*
completing   *teleutaion*
completion   *telos*
composite   *synolon*
composited   *synistamenon*
composited, be   *synistanai*
composition   *synthesis*
compound   *syntheton*
configuration   *skhēma*
contrariety   *enantiōsis*
contrary   *enantion*
corruption   *phthora*
coupled   *syndedyasmenon*

define, demarcate, determine   *horizein, diorizein*
definition   *horismos, horos*
deprivation   *sterēsis*
destructible   *phtharton*
destruction   *phthora*
determinate   *hōrismenon*
differ   *diapherein*
difference, differentia   *diaphora*
disposition   *hexis*

element   *stoikheion*
elenchus   *elenkhos*
essence   *ti ēn einai*
essence of musical   *mousikō$_i$ einai*

figure   *skhēma*
first   *prōton*
follow (logically)   *symbainein*
for the sake of   *heneka*
form (Pl., Ar.)   *eidos*
formula   *logos*

formulate   *legein*
from   *apo*
function   *ergon*

generate   *gennan*
genus   *genos*

heap   *sōros*
homonym   *homōnymon*
hoper   *hoper*

idea (Pl.)   *idea*
impossible   *adynaton*
in respect of   *kata* (acc.)
in respect of itself   *kath' hauto*
in respect of one thing   *kath' hen*
in respect of which   *kath' ho*
incapacity, inability   *adynamia*
intelligible   *noēton*

kind   *genos*
know   *gnōnai, eidenai*
knowledge   *gnōsis, epistēmē*
known   *gnōston*

lack   *sterēsis*

making   *poiēsis*
mathematika   *mathēmatika*
matter   *hylē*
move   *kinein*
movement   *kinēsis*

natural   *physikon*
nature   *physis*

nature, by *physei*

occur, obtain *hyparkhein*
of which *kath' hou*
one *hen*
origin *arkhē*
out of *ek*

participation (Pl.) *methexis*
particular *kath' hekaston*
pass-away *phtheiresthai*
peculiar *idion*
per accidens *kata symbebēkos*
perceptible *aisthēton*
perception *aisthēsis*
plurality *plēthos*
possession *hexis*
possibility, potentiality *dynamis*
possible, potential *dynaton*
posterior *hysteron*
potentially *dynamei*
predicated, be *katēgoreisthai*
predicated, thing *katēgoroumenon, katēgorēma*
primary *prōton*
principle, first principle *arkhē*
prior *proteron*
producing *poiēsis*
proper *oikeion*
purpose *heneka hou*

qua *hēi*
qualified, quality *poion*
quantified, quantity *poson*

reason (cause) *aition*

reason (given) *logos*
reason, to *noein*
reference to, in *pros*
referred to one thing *pros hen*

said, be *legesthai*
said, thing *legomenon*
say *legein*
seed *sperma*
separate *khōriston*
separated, be *khōrizesthai*
shape *morphē*
simple *haploun*
simpliciter haplōs
singular *kath' hekaston*
soul *psykhē*
species *eidos*
spontaneously *apo tautomatou*
start, start off *arkhein*
starting-point *arkhē*
subject, substrate *hypokeimenon*
substance *ousia*
suffer *paskhein*

taken together *syneilēmmenon*
tendency *hexis*
theory *logos*
think, thinking *noein, noēsis*
this, a (or some) *tode ti*
time, in *khronōi*

undergo *paskhein*
underlie *hypokeisthai*
understanding *epistēmē*
unique *idion* [*monakhon* Z 15 40^{a}29]

universal   *katholou*
universe   *ouranos* ("heaven")
unit   *hen, monas*

what it is   *ti esti*
work   *ergon*